Steve Davis
Snooker Cha

Steve Davis
Snooker Champion

His Own Story as told to Brian Radford

Pan Books London and Sydney

First published 1981 by Arthur Barker Ltd
This edition published 1983 by Pan Books Ltd,
Cavaye Place, London SW10 9PG
© Steve Davis 1981
ISBN 0 330 26864 3
Filmset in Great Britain by
Northumberland Press Ltd, Gateshead, Tyne and Wear
Printed and bound by
Hunt Barnard Ltd, Aylesbury, Bucks

With love to my mother
Jean Catherine Davis

Acknowledgements

I should like to thank my mum and dad, Dave Muscroft and the *Daily Star* for providing the photographs used in this book.

Steve Davis

Contents

Introduction

by Barry Hearn

I first met Steve Davis in March 1976, when as an eighteen-year-old he visited the Lucania Snooker Club in Romford, Essex, to play Vic Harris, then Essex amateur champion. The manager of the club asked me to come up from my office below to see the young Davis play, and it was not long before I was agreeing with his comments and those of Vic Harris that here was a very exceptional youngster indeed.

I would dearly love to say that I recognized immediately that the young Davis was a world champion in the making. Unfortunately this would be quite untrue, as my own experience of snooker had begun only two years earlier when I became the chairman of the Lucania Snooker Centre chain. What was apparent was the determination and single-mindedness in everything this lanky youngster did. Vic Harris, however, was in no doubt, and I can recall him quite clearly talking in terms of world championship prospects after just a few frames of snooker with Steve.

It was to be nearly twelve months before I really understood how good this young man was going to be. Of course, I didn't need all of that time to appreciate the finer qualities of his snooker, but simply to understand the complex character holding the cue. Snooker as a sport has always depended more on the man behind the cue than just his performance on a snooker table; the game is about character and class, for to survive in the competitive jungle of the modern-day game requires a Borg-like dedication which many talk about but only a few are prepared to offer.

In Steve's 'story' I know he has been complimentary towards everyone who has helped him during his career, and of course I am pleased to put myself in that category. I should point out immediately that many people help players in sport, but this can never be more than just a contribution towards their success. World champions are not made, but born — fate plays an enormous part in their progress to the top.

In Steve's case, one needs to look particularly at his parents for the characteristics which have become so important in his rise to the top of the snooker tree. In his father he has a demanding perfectionist, forever setting standards of only the highest quality and severe in his criticism of anything that falls short of these objectives. There can be no question that it's from Bill Davis that Steve has acquired his single-mindedness, his dedication and his strength of character. In contrast, Jean Davis displays all the charms and quiet qualities one expects to find in an infant school teacher, and from her Steve has taken the patience, the concentration and the cool, calm, collected approach he illustrates when pressure is at its peak. In a nutshell, if a character had to be invented with all the attributes necessary for a world-class sportsman, those that Steve has acquired from his parents would exactly fit the bill.

Even with these qualities, to reach the top required an enormous amount of hard work and sacrifices. For Steve's parents the sacrifices were mainly financial; but for Steve himself perhaps the greatest sacrifice of all was his teenage years. The dedication required meant that the normal teenage life of parties and discos, girlfriends and holidays simply did not exist. This was his price — which may perhaps account for the enjoyment he has now after reaching his goal!

During the late seventies the relationship between Steve and me grew from initially one of leader and follower into one of close friends, even as far as brotherly affection. His career was planned in minute detail, but only after long discussions between us about challenge match opponents, image, appearance, press coverage, etc. It was very much a joint effort, and developed into the second partnership in Steve's career – the first of course being the one with Bill Davis on learning and developing this wonderful game of snooker.

Success after success came to Steve in his amateur career, with just the occasional hiccup like the English Snooker Championship defeat in March 1978. The Lucania National title in 1977 was enough to get Steve into the England snooker team, where he was an unbeaten international, and the Pontins Open title in 1978 enabled him, on 17 September of that year, to turn professional.

From this stage, Steve's development both as a player and as a person gained momentum. His personality, like his game, became more attractive, and he continued to attract massive support from all quarters. The 'Romford Roar', that indestructible band of snooker supporters, followed him everywhere, noisily. It seemed no distance was too far for them to travel to cheer their man home. Normal working-class men, who felt so much for the talent inside this young man – one of them even risking the wrath of the Almighty by producing a banner which simply said 'Steve Davis, we worship the water you walk on'. With this support, and an enormous amount of natural talent, Steve set out on his professional career.

Strangely, his aim was not necessarily to be the world professional champion, but to be the best player in the world. Sometimes that can be the same thing, sometimes it is not. In his early career Steve and I often talked about the world title, and we agreed that while being champion of the world was essential, we were aiming at something on a far higher level, and that was for Steve to become a legend in his sport. I once heard Angelo Dundee describe the pleasures of training the one and only Muhammad Ali, and even he found the pleasure of being associated with a living legend indescribable. This attitude was my personal motivation, and I have not been disappointed.

The success of Steve's career is far better read about in his own words, but few people will appreciate the sheer pleasure of achievement more than those close to Steve who have seen exactly what he has gone through to achieve his goals.

After the tears had dried and heart-beats returned to near normality in Sheffield on 20 April 1981, the most amazing thing was that the young man holding the trophy was still in every respect the same person who had first walked into my snooker club five years earlier. His hair was shorter now, the clothes better, the personality perhaps a little more outward, but the character, professionalism and beliefs have all remained the same.

For me, Steve Davis the person is best summed up by a remark made by him some months after winning the world championship and receiving the acclaim reserved for superstar sportsmen, when he said, 'I've tried being flash, but I'm afraid I'm not very good at it.' Steve Davis the person is still, and will remain, bigger than Steve Davis the superstar, and for this reason alone a new chapter in the history of snooker is in the process of being written.

1 My Dad and Joe's Bible

Whatever I achieve in my career as a snooker player, I will always owe a large part of it to my father, Bill, and to my manager and best friend, Barry Hearn.

Why they call him Bill, my mother and I have no idea for it states quite clearly in his birth certificate that he was registered as plain Harry George. From the very beginning, in my great love for snooker, dad has been my teacher, my biggest supporter and my sternest critic all rolled into one. And he still is today.

There was a strange element of luck about the way it all began, and even now we can hardly believe that the huge, impossible dream has really come true.

At first, dad was a darts fanatic at heart. He played for a club team and took the game seriously. He takes most things seriously. So seriously in the case of darts that he developed the dreaded 'freeze'. Every time he went up to throw, the dart just stayed in his hand.

This embarrassed him a lot, for dad takes so much pride in all he does. Though I must confess I'm delighted it happened – or I might be going round with a beer-gut today!

On failing to beat the 'freeze', dad was forced to find a new game to play, because he enjoys club life so much. Snooker was the obvious answer. The only trouble was, he didn't know how to play the game properly. He could handle a cue and pot a ball, but that wasn't enough. Playing just for fun didn't interest him. He either played seriously, or not at all.

So to solve his problem he went straight out and bought

the incomparable Joe Davis manual. The bible. The best textbook ever written on the game, although mine's out soon and should give it a run. Almost overnight, dad developed an obsession in the skills that Joe said were needed to reach a respectable standard in the game. He fell in love with snooker in the same way that I did some years later.

Joe was virtually invincible. Anyone who can remain undisputed world champion for twenty years must be special. He was the first man to foresee a future for snooker as a game in its own right. Until he came along, it was mainly regarded as a party piece to wind up an evening of billiards.

Joe had vision. He saw the game's potential. He realized it required more accuracy than billiards, and he concentrated on technique, which acccounted for his book being accepted by players of all standards as the undisputed bible.

With great devotion, dad would open up the book at one particular section and struggle on for days to perfect his technique and try to achieve what Joe had said was ultimately possible. But, no matter how hard dad tried, and no matter how much time and effort he put in, he just couldn't master the game. He couldn't transform Joe's words into shots. Perhaps he started too late. As the years went by, dad became a good-class club player but had to accept that he could improve no more, and began to pay more attention to me.

I was born at St Nicholas Hospital in Plumstead, South-East London, on 22 August 1957, which makes me a Leo – just! Perhaps this might account for my red mane, although some people reckon I'm such a perfectionist at snooker that there's a bit of a Virgo in me, too.

With dad nuts about snooker, I didn't have to wait long for a table. I was just two when mum paid two pounds for a toy one at Woolworth's as a Christmas present.

To call it a snooker table was a joke. It was just a flimsy strip of hardboard, three feet in length and a foot and a half wide. Six blocks of wood were nailed around the sides to stop the balls falling off, and six pieces of rubber were glued fast to act as cushions. The cues were merely two short sticks with no tips. Worse still, the table was sold with only billiard balls, and mum wanted me to play snooker – just like dad!

Then, magic, mum had a brainwave. She took an old string of wooden beads from a drawer, cut them free, and spent the whole of Christmas Day patiently painting them one by one into a complete snooker set.

The toy board, which was small enough to fit on our coffee table, was about hip high to me and I toddled around it, trying hard to prod the beads into the cotton pockets. It amused me for hours, though I'm still convinced it was bought as much for dad to play on as it was for me.

My first memory of a full-sized table remains particularly vivid. I was five at the time, and dad had taken me to watch him play at his Lee Green Workingmen's club in South-east London. The balls fascinated me so much I got up from my seat, stretched over the table and picked up the black – to howls of protest from everyone in sight. Fortunately this didn't frighten me off snooker forever. In fact my fascination continued.

I enjoyed school life from the start and became keen on all sports, especially football. Every Saturday, from seven upwards, I went along to support Charlton Athletic, my local club. One of their players, Keith Peacock, later coached me at the Alexandra McLeod Junior School in Abbey Wood, and, strangely enough, presented me with my first cue-case as a prize for being the most promising player at the Plumstead Common Workingmen's Club.

Someone must have been impressed with my skills as a right-winger, because when I was ten I was chosen for the Woolwich and district schools' side. Then, on the day before the match, I went down with flu and the doctor ordered me to stay in bed. All my hopes of becoming England's second Stanley Matthews were destroyed by a red card from the doctor, strictly enforced by my mum.

I enjoyed cricket, too, but only as a bowler. I hated batting. Facing fast bowlers didn't appeal to me as sport, though I thought I was better than Boycott with a tennis ball!

Every now and again I would watch dad play at the club, and as my toy table had long since worn out by the time I was eight, I wanted a new one.

Mum again produced it as a Christmas present, and by some strange coincidence this one, too, came without snooker balls. The makers packed them in a long cardboard box, but on their way from the factory they became separated from the table and were lost. Mum thought she would have to rummage through the drawers again for more beads, but dad went down to the railway station and found them among the parcels.

This new table, a Joe Davis one, was five feet in length and two and a half feet wide. Amply big enough for me, and certainly big enough for our tiny kitchen, the only room in our flat that could accommodate it without the furniture getting wrecked and the ornaments smashed.

To be able to play, I had to put it on top of the kitchen table and push the lot against a wall.

I used to mess about on it a good deal. One day I decided to see how many times a ball would go up and down on the table, and in trying to break the record, I rolled it too hard and it flew over the side and smashed the kitchen window.

Knowing dad would be furious if he found out, mum tried to cover up for me. She bought some putty and a new pane and asked the man next door if he would put it in for us before dad came home from work.

As soon as he opened the door, dad smelt the putty and the game was up – and so was my table, inside the cupboard, against the wall! He said the table had to be put away until I learnt to behave myself.

'If you can't play seriously, then don't play at all!' he said.

After all this trouble, I lost interest in the table. For a

brief spell I took up smoking, though I'm not sure whether mum and dad ever knew about it. I only did it to be like the gang in school, coughing my lungs up behind the bicycle shed. It all ended as sharply as it began. I was kicked out of the gang and I threw the cigarettes in the gutter, and I haven't smoked since.

I was a week or two past my fourteenth birthday when I first played on a full-size table. The whole family went on holiday to a camp at St Mary's Bay in Kent, and before we had time to open our bags, dad was rushing off in search of the snooker-room. As soon as I saw the table, my interest perked up again. We had booked in for a fortnight, so, for the first time in my life, dad was able to teach me properly, and I spent a whole week doing nothing but learning the basic techniques of the game. He could see I was loving every minute of it. Being able to play on a full-size table rekindled my enthusiasm. We practically lived in the snooker-room, and for the first time I began to understand what excitement the game could offer.

Dad entered a competition they were holding during the week and proceeded to win it. There were no cash prizes, just a Thermos flask! I was excited, and asked to enter myself in the second week. I even had visions of winning.

My first ever opponent was an old man, who took particular delight in snookering me whenever he could. He played lots and lots of safety shots, always muttering 'Snooker's the name of the game . . .' I was annihilated.

Having set my heart on playing my father in the final, I was very depressed at losing. I left the room with tears in my eyes. I felt I had let myself down, and let dad down. Given the chance, I'd probably beat that man with one hand now.

In time, dad came along and talked some common sense to me and tried to cheer me up.

After our chat, dad got up and winked at me, saying, 'Don't worry, Steve, I'll go off and beat him for us.'

In fact, he not only thrashed him, but went on to win his second Thermos in a fortnight, so instead of celebrating with champagne, we drank hot tea all the way home.

At fourteen, I was now old enough to realize how skilful snooker really was, and having played on a full-size table for the first time, I was determined to learn everything I could about the game.

As soon as we reached home, I went straight to the Joe Davis book and started reading it. Dad was delighted, and he promised to take me to his club to play, provided the committee would let me on the tables. Because dad was in the team, they gave him the nod and made a special concession for me, although I was still too young to be a member.

I enjoyed instant success at the club. I knocked up my first thirty break after only a few weeks there, although I didn't have a cue of my own and had to borrow one from the rack.

Having recorded this thirty break, dad and I decided it was time to have my own cue, and we went up to London and chose one for fifteen pounds. We bought it on a Saturday morning and rushed back to the club to test it out. It was disastrous. I just couldn't hit the ball straight. Time and time again, I kept going in-off. I was very upset, and realized then that snooker was all about players and ability and had nothing to do with cues, particularly as this new one was dead straight, and far superior to the ones in the club.

All of a sudden snooker had taken me over. I could think of nothing else. I couldn't learn enough or play enough. The quarter-size table was forever coming out in the kitchen. We were so cramped for space that I could only play properly from one end.

It was hell for mum. She kept complaining that I stopped her from getting to the cooker and the cupboards, and that she couldn't serve a meal because the table was never free. The only greens she saw in those days were on their way to the pockets!

Every time dad and I played together, he made sure I kept to *the* book. And there was never any scoring. Just coaching, coaching all the time. Dad reckoned that trying to score points could be a distraction. As always, he was a stickler for absolute and undivided concentration. He was determined to see that I first learned the correct physical techniques before I went on to the much harder departments of the game. A simple case of learning to 'walk before you run. Despite dad's conservative approach, my great love affair with snooker had begun.

We enjoyed a marvellous rapport – as soon as I learned to admit when I was wrong about something I did, which wasn't very easy. I often became moody during those practice sessions. Like most fourteen-year-olds, I didn't relish being told what to do, and we had a few arguments. Then I'd go away and sleep on it and realize that maybe dad was right, and all was forgiven and forgotten in the morning.

From the start, dad was adamant that I should not develop bad habits. He was obsessed with technique. It was the basis of my game. That's why the Joe Davis manual was so important to both of us. All I did for three years was learn, learn, learn. Grafting hard, with dad insisting that I should be close to perfection all the time in all I did. Some lads of my age might have found the hours of practice tediously repetitive, but I lapped up every minute of it, and would have welcomed more.

Without ever dreaming of what the future held in store for us, dad and I got down to tackling the game of snooker with a dedication which, even then, must have bordered on the professional.

The little table, on which I brushed up the lessons dad gave me at the club, was totally indestructible. Several times it threatened to break up, but mum or dad always came to the rescue. Mum sewed up the pockets so often, we lost count, and when the cloth wore out, dad brought an old piece home from the club and stuck it down.

We got our money's worth from that table. It cost my parents thirty pounds, which was a lot for them in those days. I was eight when they bought it, shortly after my brother Keith was born, and it lasted me eight years. I grew out of it in the end and, as Keith was showing no interest in the game at that stage, dad sold it to a friend. It's probably still going strong today.

Dad was an average player, but good for the area. He never pretended to be better. Technically, he was virtually perfect. He always knew what should be done, and the way to go about it, but he lacked that vital bit of natural talent that would enable him to put it together on the table, which was obviously where it mattered.

As long as I can remember, he's been a maniac about snooker. Joe Davis had retired when dad took up the game, and John Pulman was champion. He was the hero. Dad regarded John as the best technician in the business, though Fred Davis must also have impressed him, because one night he came home boasting he had his autograph for me.

Mum is keen on the game, too, but she has never played it. She is one of my most loyal supporters and, given the chance, wouldn't miss a single match in which I played.

Dad and I were very disappointed when the Lee Green club amazingly decided to sell one of their two tables to make room for a lounge. We were disgusted. He was left with no alternative but to leave them – after years of playing in the team – and find somewhere new.

With dad on the transfer list, several clubs were soon hot on his trail. He went to see them all one by one, and decided in the end that Plumstead Common Workingmen's had the best facilities by far. Yet even then he refused to commit himself to them until they agreed to let me play on the tables whenever they were free. They had four in all. These snooker conditions were far better than anything else I had come across. True to their word, the club allowed me to play, although I was still much too young to be a member. As far as I'm concerned this was the best move dad ever made. The club gave us a wonderful welcome and my whole game burst into life overnight.

With tables available, and living a lot closer, I travelled down to the club several evenings in the week and become absolutely hooked on practice. Now that we had the chance to play on the tables regularly, dad immediately stepped up on the essential basic principles of the game, and not a minute was wasted.

There were still times when we got on each other's nerves, mainly because dad would see my mistakes and found it frustrating when I couldn't put them right. However, I wanted to learn and he wanted to teach me, and surely there could not have been any better prescription for a successful relationship between us.

Though I lost interest in most other sports, I remained keen on chess. Dad played the game during lunchtimes at work, and we'd sort out a few moves in the evenings for him to try on his mates next day. As with snooker, dad taught me how to understand chess at an early age, and I became the best player in school – if you didn't include my maths master.

Without a break, dad and I continued to follow the Joe Davis book, but he thought I might benefit from a visit to Jack Karnehm to make sure I was being taught in the proper way. Jack is a world-class billiards player, and a knowledge-able BBC commentator on snooker.

Dad thought a second opinion would be useful, and had been told Jack was a good tutor. Dad paid three pounds an hour for me to see him, and I went twice for two hours at a time.

Jack was most impressed with my technique, but spotted a few flaws that dad and I had overlooked. In particular, Jack advised me to play billiards more, along with my snooker. Over the years, it has proved a useful tip and has helped me a lot to understand the complex skills of snooker, as billiards is a game where control of the white ball is essential.

There was no doubt that Jack realized my potential. He wanted to see me every week, but as a family we couldn't afford it.

One important piece of advice from Jack concerned the way I was hitting the cue-ball. He noticed that I was playing my shots without actually being aware of the exact spot that I was striking on the ball. To correct this fault, I practised for hours, simply hitting the white ball up and down the table, watching it pass over the spots on the way up before striking the top cushion and then watching it pass over the spots again on the way back. Said quickly, it might sound easy. It is not. It can drive you insane! A boring, but important exercise and one which proves that a player is capable of striking the cue-ball in the centre.

In another practice routine, I would pot all the colours off their spots and then, before potting the black, would re-spot the colours and try to gain position on the yellow, carrying on the process over and over again to see how many times I could do it without missing. My best ever in later years was thirteen, before I stopped, deciding I had mastered it.

Because of Jack's advice, I stepped up on my billiards and as one of the Plumstead Common tables was set aside exclusively for the game, I was able to work hard at it.

To put myself to the test, I entered the Under-19 British snooker and billiards championships, with the first round in Essex. I was sixteen at the time, and played Paul Smith, a useful performer when you consider that he is badly handicapped with the loss of an eye. This was my first proper tournament, apart from the one at the holiday camp, and I had no complaints when he beat me 3–2, particularly as he had knocked up a fifty-nine break in the match before ours. I actually had a chance to beat him 3–1, but I missed a red with the long rest and it cost me the fourth frame. Later that day Paul completed the double over me, winning the billiards event as well.

Paul does a marvellous impression of Ray Reardon. I played him in a one-frame exhibition match at Luton shortly after winning the world title and he murdered me. He looked more like Reardon than Reardon himself!

After being knocked out of the Under-19 championships, I soon found some comfort back at the club when I rattled up my first fifty break at snooker. To make it even more pleasant, I scored it against the club's best player, Bert Steele, the man who, at that time, I had set my sights on to beat.

Dad and I were still not sure how far I could go. A chap called Roy Connors came to the club, and later, after watching him play, dad said, 'You must realize you'll never be as good as him.' Deep inside, I remember thinking, 'I don't see why not.'

It wasn't that dad doubted my potential, he was just concerned that I wasn't getting the strongest type of opposition to improve my play.

Being advised to concentrate more on billiards, I would nip off during any free time at school to brush up on my game at the club. It was there that I met Dick Sharples, a kindly old man and the only person to make a century in the place at billiards. As his sight was failing, he had given up playing and taken the job of brushing and ironing the tables and re-tipping the cues. He knew both games well. He watched me practise at billiards and taught me many shots.

Every so often, he would bring out his cue and demonstrate a few shots with it on the table. The cue was his prize possession. Perhaps a bit thick at the tip, but a lovely piece of wood all the same. Looking back on those days, it is now obvious that he longed for me to have it, but it didn't impress me any more than the one I had. Then, right out of the blue, dad came home and said, 'I've got a present for you.'

Dick Sharples had insisted that dad took the cue home for me. He told him he wanted me and no one else to have it – and, strangely enough, a month or so later he died. Perhaps he knew his days were numbered, and if they can get BBC television way up there behind the pearly gates, I bet he was cheering his heart out when I won the world title.

It was terribly sad when he died, but I've stuck by that cue and it's never let me down. It never leaves my side. It's the tool of my trade. I care for it in the same way as Boycott cares for his bats and Borg his rackets.

I can't say I showed the same respect for my first one, though. I had a habit of biting the cue in anger and frustration if I played a bad shot. So if anyone is going round with a cue that has rows and rows of teeth-marks around the splicing, then it's probably the one that first put me on the road.

Actually a lot of rubbish is talked about cues. It's all a matter of getting used to the one you own. There are no hard and fast rules. I just accept mine as a cue. A beginner might be wise to choose one that is straight, with an average tip of ten millimetres and a weight of around seventeen ounces, which is roughly the same as mine.

In time, a cue becomes part of you. Alex Higgins has one that's as stiff as a poker; Terry Griffiths has one that's thin and whippy; and John Spencer's first cue was nothing more than a bent lump of wood with a nail through the butt. With a cue, it's all a matter of confidence.

Snooker fascinated me right through my teens, but I took great care not to let it interfere with my studies. By now, I had started my 'O' levels course and realized that education and good qualifications were important to me.

In the end, I came away with a handful of 'O's in physics, French, maths, English literature and English language. Every Monday morning the French teacher would ask me what I did at the weekend, and I would reply, 'J'ai joué au snooker.' It became a ritual.

Going on for 'A' levels in physics and maths appealed to me for a short while and I worked hard for a couple of months before I accepted that snooker was all I cared about. If there'd been an 'A' level in snooker, I'd have been the teacher!

To earn some pocket-money to pay for my snooker, I took a weekend job in a butcher's department in a supermarket. I worked a ten-hour shift for a miserable three pounds, but had some good laughs, although being locked in the freezer every Saturday afternoon wasn't one of them.

Very few months went by at this stage without my mother – a teacher in an infants' class – asking me what job I had in mind for when I left school. I had no idea. All I could think of was snooker, yet when I finally left at the age of nineteen, it had still not clicked that I would eventually end up as a professional player.

My game continued to improve and my top break rose steadily through the sixties to the eighties until, while playing Dave Clissold at the Plumstead Common club, on 2 January 1975, the magic century arrived. I remember nervously potting the pink to make the break 102, with the last red fairly near the middle pocket, and the white ball close to the top cushion. I potted the red, but the white ball travelled down the table, kissed the yellow which was on its spot, and disastrously went in-off. Mind you, I wasn't bothered as I knew I had reached a personal milestone.

A further eight months slipped by before I scored my next century. But I was still only seventeen, and it proved that my game was definitely on the upgrade.

On reaching eighteen, I was chosen to represent the Plumstead Common club both in billiards and snooker. The teams were made up of the best players in the club, and no one knew his opponent until match night, when lots were drawn from a hat.

Although my reputation as a rising star was going ahead of me around the clubs, there were still one or two players who had not heard of my name and this led to several funny incidents.

Before one billiards match, the names came out of the hat in the usual way and the man who drew me was so excited at landing a youngster that he rushed off to tell his non-playing captain sitting in another room.

As it happened, the games captain knew all about me, but he decided to keep quiet, knowing full well how the match would go once I got his man on the table.

Three shots later, I had reached my allotted 150 points, which included a century break. Stunned by this defeat from a lanky kid, my opponent crept back to his games captain with the proverbial egg dripping all over his face.

On another night, and again playing billiards, I was drawn against a small, funny-looking man with glasses and a pipe. He didn't own a cue, so he selected one from the club rack. Then he proceeded to chalk the end vigorously for a minute or more – until someone told him the cue had no tip!

Not embarrassed a bit, he then looked around for another cue. Eventually he found what he thought was a cue but, in fact, was the club's six-foot half-butt. No one told him it wasn't a proper cue so without realizing what he had in his hand, he played the whole game with a half-butt. He was such a weird chap that during the match he picked up one of the whites to see whether it was his, with the spot on it. This, of course, was a foul, and it reduced everyone in the hall to tears.

Then, to top it all, instead of getting out the rest to play an awkward shot, he decided on a flash one. Pipe in mouth, he placed the cue behind his back, missed the red by a mile and reduced us to dribbling on the floor. I ended up laughing so much that I walked from the room with a handkerchief in my mouth.

The incidents weren't always funny, of course. One night while playing for the club I came up against a fairly good player in his forties who was furious because I kept potting his white ball.

Halfway through the game, he left the table to speak to his son, a huge lad with long hair, and a leading candidate for Yob of the Year. In an obvious attempt to scare the pants off me, the son came up to the table and, with a clear threat in his voice, said, 'Hey, you, why do you keep potting my dad's white, then?'

I completely ignored him and potted the white even more to annoy them both.

Lots of laymen believe it is bad etiquette to pot an opponent's ball. Well, it's not. It's just the same as laying a snooker.

There was a moral in these club games, too. I obtained my first lesson in the dangers of becoming over-confident. Several opponents beat me who didn't have my ability, and I lost games simply through not concentrating hard enough, and from taking matters too casually. Such bad habits breed complacency and that, for me, is the worst crime of all.

One of my biggest disappointments around this time was losing 4–2 in the English amateur championships to Brian Tressider. I had just turned eighteen, and I really believed I should have won. But you have to lose before you win, and I'm a firm believer in the theory that you learn more from losing than from winning. Often experience is as important as skill.

Competitions are all about winning and losing, and it is imperative that a player accepts both gracefully and never lets the occasion change him from the person he really is.

Playing in the clubs inevitably brought me into contact with drink, although the most I could manage was the occasional lager. I remember a night when I went to support John Smith from the Plumstead Common club in the national CIU tournament at Welwyn Garden City.

Twelve of us hired a mini-bus to give John a good cheer, but he lost 3–0. Still, it made no difference to the booze-up afterwards. Drinks came pouring in from all angles, and I was soon going well above my limit. I remember drinking four pints of light ale and four Scotches. We were in a hall and a cabaret was going on. When I had put away my fourth Scotch, I looked up at the compere and saw *two* of him! For the first time in my life I had double vision.

The spotlight swung towards us and the compere congratulated us on being the best supporters in the world for taking our defeat so well. The words had barely left his lips when I sprinted through the door and was violently sick.

I felt rotten – but not half as bad as John Smith. He had such a good time that on the way home he finished up lying on the mini-bus floor with his head out of the back door doing an impression of an extra exhaust-system, leaving a revolting trail all along the white line.

It seems the public at large believe that I am an innocent teetotaller. This is not so. I enjoy wine with a meal and a lager with a curry, but I rarely, if ever, go out just to drink. And I have one very definite and strict rule. I never touch a drop of any alcohol when I'm engaged in a game of snooker.

Having tried twice in the junior championships, I entered in my last year and was drawn to meet Tony Meo at Ron Gross's club in Neasden, in the first of our many battles.

Someone had warned me that Tony was an exceptional player and arguments buzzed through the club that day about which of us would win. On this occasion, I overpowered him 3–1 and I qualified for the final stages at Jim Williamson's Northern Snooker Centre in Leeds.

I played Tony on Grand National Day, and we were warned before the start that when the race began we would be asked to stop playing, as much in our interests as everyone else's. I was going nicely on a break when someone called a halt and switched on the telly.

As it turned out, I drew the second horse in the Sweep, so I didn't feel too sore when told I could go on with my break.

It was while playing Tony at Neasden that I first saw his friend Jimmy White. He was just twelve then. He had broken his leg and was playing shots with his walking-stick. And I must admit there have been a few times since when I've wished he was still playing with it.

I then travelled up to Leeds, where I reached the semi-finals of the snooker championships only to lose 4–2 to Ian Williamson. Although disappointed, having set my sights on the snooker title, revenge was swift and sweet when I beat Ian in the final of the billiards championships just three hours later, to secure my first national title.

During those early days, I won the Northern area Kent billiards and snooker finals three years in a row. They paid me twenty pounds for winning at snooker, another twenty for the billiards, and three pounds for the highest break. After the third year, they got tired of my going off with the cash and said there would only be prizes in future. As we didn't want more Thermos flasks in the family, that was the last they saw of me.

2 Lucky Break at Lucania

I was eighteen when I finally decided there was no point in staying on at school. My mother was a bit worried because there seemed little hope of finding a job without a pocketful of 'A' levels. Academically, I was regarded as 'bright' and was in the top stream at the Comprehensive.

When I told my mother I was coming out of school, she went along to the local council and obtained an application form for a clerical appointment in the finance department. Then she called at Barclays to see whether they had a job for me.

It hadn't dawned on mum that a career in snooker was the obvious and natural choice for me – and come to that, it hadn't dawned on me either!

Dad, however, realized that I was still improving at snooker and gave me the chance of a lifetime by offering me a year to prove myself.

By now, he was taking me around the clubs to see the best players in action. One night we went to the Southall Conservative Club, but their so-called talent scout wasn't very impressed. He reckoned I lacked flair and style, and was certain I didn't have the necessary qualities to go far in the game.

Around the same time, we went to the New Eltham Social Club to watch an exhibition match that involved professionals David Taylor, Marcus Owen and Patsy Houlihan, and amateur John Beech, the CIU champion of that year.

Marcus Owen won the event, and at the bar later one

of my friends pointed to me and said, 'You want to watch out for this kid, he's getting good.'

So Marcus put down his drink, glanced at me and said, 'You might do well, but you don't look like a snooker player.' He was obviously referring to my shape, for I was very thin and lanky.

Still, my shape didn't put him off entirely because he invited me over to the Leyton Midland Club, where he was based. This was a man who at one stage was the most feared of all London professionals and considered by some pundits as the best player in the world. I was thrilled by this offer, and I gave him no chance to change his mind. The very next morning, with cue and cash in my hand, I set off by bus to his club. I had no job and depended largely on my mother and father to help pay my expenses. To reach the 'Midland' I needed two bus trips, which took an hour and a half.

The club itself was a dump, squeezed tightly into a narrow arch under a railway line. Five tables were crammed into the room downstairs, and I was told a further two tables could be found upstairs. The place was so eerie, I never went up to find out.

It was the first real experience of leaving my little domain in Plumstead Common and going out into the big wide world. The Midland was full of shrewd, funny characters, but I remember it best for the way it literally shook every time a train went over the top, and how the water dripped down the walls when it rained.

Against all this, it served the best cheese-rolls I've ever tasted, and for weeks on end I virtually lived on them.

I always played on the number one table. Facing it, along the wall was a seat for four, filled every day with the same staring eyes. No one dared move from his seat, even for a cup of tea, or his place would be lost. I learned this to my expense when a cheese-roll jumped up from twenty pence to the cost of a seat.

At the Leyton Midland, we played a game called Points.

Usually four people playing one after the other as individuals, and with each player earning two and a half pence for every point scored in a frame. They gave me a small start at first, but this soon disappeared.

My exit from the Midland was as swift as my arrival. One afternoon I knocked up a break of ninety and within half an hour had made another of ninety-nine. It proved a good pay-day. The unwritten rules of Points state that the person who played immediately before the man who made the break is entirely responsible for settling the account. Not surprisingly, hints were dropped that I had become too good for the school.

I was nearing nineteen at the time and already with six century breaks to my credit. Yet if anyone had predicted then that in just five years I would be lifting the world professional snooker trophy over my head, I would have called them crazy.

On leaving the Midland, I remembered an occasion several months earlier when Les Coates, manager of the Romford Lucania, played at the Plumstead Common club and said I should go to Romford and test my talents against their top man Vic Harris.

The name Vic Harris didn't mean much to me at the time, but when I heard that he had whitewashed Wally Broomfield, a top player at the Midland, by three games to nil, I knew he must be a bit special. In beating Wally on his home patch, Vic made a marvellous century. As I'd never made a hundred on that table, I realized I should be accepting Les Coates's advice and testing the strength of this man Harris.

So, on leaving the Midland, I made straight for Romford, an even longer bus trip from home. I walked excitedly up the stairs into the Lucania and was instantly recognized by Les Coates.

He told me Vic was a lorry driver, but never missed his two o'clock game of snooker. He was right. Vic walked in bang on time and we shook hands and had our first game.

After the first few frames, we stopped playing seriously and played in a more relaxed manner, chatting about various shots and discussing the game in general.

At no time, in all the years that I've known Vic Harris, have I heard one bad word spoken against him. He is a wonderful abassador for the game. Vic had been Essex champion four times when I first met him, and was acknowledged as one of the finest amateurs in the whole of Britain.

I played Vic three afternoons a week and it wasn't long before he suggested that I should enter for the Lucania national competition, which is always held in September.

To press my claim, Vic went off to see Barry Hearn, who organized the tournament. He asked him to come up from his office downstairs to see how well I played. I now know he fairly raved about my prospects in the game.

Barry was comparatively new to snooker. A chartered accountant by profession, and one of the youngest ever to qualify for the Fellowship. He became chairman of Lucania Snooker Clubs in 1974.

As soon as he walked through the door, providence smiled on me. Barry saw me play a difficult four-cushion shot to get out of a tricky snooker which Vic had manufactured. It was a shot that has remained in Barry's mind ever since, though I can't say I remember it in detail myself.

I now know that when Vic first pointed me out to Barry, he quickly noticed that I had ginger hair! I've found out since that Barry, for some reason, finds it hard to get on with ginger-haired people, though I've fortunately proved to be the exception.

Barry complimented me on the shot and our friendship grew from that moment. He introduced me to his lovely wife, Susan, and in time I became one of the family. They now have two children, Katie and Edward. I'm his godfather – lucky chap!

In time, Barry was to become my manager, adviser, accountant and everything you would want in a good friend.

As a tiny coincidence, about five years after I first met Vic, he won the English amateur championships and promptly turned professional, joining me under Barry's expert management.

When we first met, Barry and I were poles apart as people. He was always bustling with great confidence, and I was still very shy and quiet.

I told Barry that I was keen to take part in the Lucania championships. Up to five hundred pounds could be won, and this alone was an attractive incentive. Barry apologized and explained that the competition was kept strictly to members of his twenty Lucania clubs, and that he wouldn't bend the rules for anyone, pointing out that I had just started at Romford. He wanted to keep out the sharks, and felt this was a good way of returning money to those who had provided it in the first place.

Though disappointed, I told Barry I wanted to play at the Romford club at least twice a week, and that if anyone dropped out of the tournament, I hoped he would give me the first option to step in. Barry agreed, and for the next few months I kept my fingers crossed that the chance would come, continuing to travel across the river to play Vic and the lads.

My improvement at this stage was astounding even me. Word was going around Romford that I was quickly catching up with Vic and, although no money ever changed hands between us, we occasionally played the best of five for a cup of tea and a Mars bar.

Not only was my game sharpening up, my personality was developing too. Romford people are renowned for their micky-taking and, at that time, I had absolutely no ammunition to defend myself. In the nicest way, Vic was a past master in the art of winding people up, and he gave me and many other people sheer hell. In particular he took great pleasure in stirring me up over my hair which, in those days, dropped down to my shoulders. He'd embarrass me so much, I'd go bright red.

It wasn't just me he made fun of, though. He used to come to the club from work with tears rolling down his face as he recalled how he'd just taken the micky out of his works manager, probably the only man on earth who didn't get on with him.

In the end, I had no alternative but to find ways of hitting back at him. I remember saying, 'Vic, you must be the only guy in the world who could put three billiard balls in his mouth and still not get a cannon!' Hardly original, but effective.

Almost without noticing, my personality began to develop at the same rate as my snooker. To survive at Romford, playing well wasn't enough. You needed a bit of lip, too! Gradually my confidence grew and I felt more at home, and a genuine member of the crowd.

Little did I realize it at the time, but all that Romford banter was to help me a lot in later years when it came to exchanging words with hecklers at exhibition matches.

When I wasn't at Romford, dad was still coaching me up at the Plumstead Common club, particularly at weekends; still correcting the faults, and still suffering the same arguments. It was very important for the coaching to continue and to ensure that any bad habits were kept at bay. It is something we still do today.

All through those first few months at Romford, I continued to hope for some good news about the tournament. With my game improving so rapidly, I knew I could do myself justice provided I got the chance. Barry knew how I felt, but he refused to give way. He was a man of his word. Then suddenly, right out of the blue, came the slice of luck I needed so much. Paul Smith found that he couldn't be released from work, and scratched from the tournament. Barry told me straightaway, and I was seeded number six.

Every one of the twenty Lucania clubs sent its top players to the final and backed them up to the hilt with hordes of enthusiastic supporters. They converged on Romford in their droves and were all crammed into the club for a 10.30 morning start.

Altogether, eight tables were in action, with the matches decided on the best of three frames, and with the final played over five. It was by far the biggest competition I had played. The excitement of it all keyed me up, and made me determined to do well.

With plenty of care through the day, I managed to reach the quarter-finals and came up against none other than Vic Harris whom I saw as my next step up the ladder. This definitely went down as Match of the Day. It was the one the packed hall had been waiting for, to see whether I could beat him.

As you'd expect, the tension was tremendous. I considered Vic just slightly the favourite, but after sharing the first two frames, it was obviously anyone's game as we started the decider.

From the beginning of that final frame, it was always a close, nerve-testing encounter with neither of us pulling away. With one red left, it was still anyone's match. Vic potted the red and took the black to go twenty-three points in front. He had a good position on the yellow and it looked a straightforward pot. Frankly, I had already accepted defeat. But nothing in snooker is ever a foregone conclusion, no matter how easy a shot might seem to the public.

Top professionals in particular find themselves wide open to criticism in this respect. In putting screw, stun or 'side' on the cue-ball, with a view to finding a good position for the next shot, they occasionally miss what might seem to be a simple pot – and the people watching can't believe their eyes. I've experienced this situation more times than I'd care to remember.

Amazingly, Vic missed the yellow, but enjoyed some luck as the colour rolled into a safe position. But his luck didn't last much longer. I followed up with a safety shot, only this time – to Vic's horror – the yellow trickled across the table, struck the brown, and fluked its way into the middle pocket. With all the other colours in easy, potable positions, I had no trouble in cleaning them up to win the match 2–1 and enter the semi-finals.

To eliminate Vic, albeit with a slice of luck, gave me great confidence. I was buzzing. Just Wally West, of the Hounslow Lucania, now stood between me and a place in the final. He presented no problem and I beat him 2–0 in a canter. Wally West is typical of so many capable players who have enormous potential, but often fail to produce the goods under pressure in matches.

Defending champion Geoff Foulds was my illustrious opponent in the final. A hard match-player, and someone with immense patience who will wait and wait until his opponent gets careless and lets him in. As it turned out, Geoff's overall experience proved too much for me, and I lost graciously by three frames to one.

There were few regrets, though, because this was a big day for me. Just to play in the competition, after all the anxious waiting, was a wonderful thrill, so to reach the final could only be classed as a bonus. However, my performance probably hindered Vic's progress in the club, because I now took over from him as Romford's top dog.

An envelope containing the runner-up's prize-money of £260 made me feel like a Pools winner. A further reward came in the shape of Lucania sponsorship, which Barry decided should be a tour of England with all expenses paid.

3 Have Cue, Will Travel

Being successful in the Lucania championships was considered a definite stepping-stone towards the English amateur team. I wasn't so conceited as to think I was ready to stake a claim on the strength of one performance, but I was sensible enough to understand that the spotlight could be swung in my direction, and that my chances shouldn't be ruled out altogether. I really hoped I'd be picked, because I considered it a great honour to play for my country.

Against this feeling of hope, I realized that players in the north were usually looked on more favourably for international places than those based in the south. Players who had been in the game much longer than myself blamed the bias on administrators who lived in the north and preferred to select men from their own area, irrespective of the form being shown by players in the south.

This type of prejudice bothered Barry a lot, and he longed to pick a side from the south to go up north to challenge the best on their tables. He did, in fact, put together a Lucania representative side, but the only challenge he got came from the Pot Black club in Clapham. Needless to say, with a £500 sidestake riding on the match, the Lucania team won convincingly!

Eventually Barry organized a national tour in which Geoff Foulds and I took part together and played against most of the leading amateurs.

He deliberately put together a tough schedule to see how well we could stand up to all the travelling, and to the pressure of playing matches every night.

Our first port of call was Grimsby where I sailed in against Mike Hallett, an exciting player who later turned professional.

From Grimsby we travelled on to Hull and then to Edinburgh, with Geoff doing all the driving in a hired car. I had passed my test, but the insurance didn't cover me in this case. There was hardly time to grab a haggis before we were setting off on a 250-mile journey to Dudley in the midlands.

Already my knowledge of north country dialect was beginning to prosper. In just three days I had learnt two different ways of referring to a frame. In Grimsby they called it a 'set', and in Edinburgh it was an 'angle'. Even more curiously, in Grimsby they kept calling the table a 'board'.

By now the car was coughing and sneezing and obviously homesick. Because the carburettor was on the blink, we couldn't go faster than forty miles an hour on the motorway, and it took us all of ten hours to crawl from Edinburgh to our hotel in Dudley. It was no surprise when we both lost our matches and we wound our weary way back to our beds. We were both shattered, and I remember the night porter, like an extra from a horror film, being asked by Geoff if there was any 'danger' of having a cup of tea.

A new carburettor was fitted in the morning and we drove back up north to Bolton, where we were slaughtered 8–0 by Tony Knowles and Stan Haslam. Geoff was now cheesed off. On top of all the problems with the car, he was worried about his wife at home being put under pressure by builders supplying the finishing touches to an extension.

He definitely didn't fancy a return trip to the midlands to play in Birmingham. His loyalties were split between home and tour. He had reached the crossroads. I wasn't entirely happy either, having sampled my first – and last – taste of black pudding and used up a whole tube of toothpaste to bring things back to normal.

Barry came up from London for the Birmingham match, and Geoff told him he would like to pull out. Barry accepted the situation, but as he could see I was keen to continue, he said he'd like the tour to go on. Before the night was out, he had telephoned Russell Jarmak at home in Kent and arranged for him to replace Geoff who was allowed to drop out.

With Geoff taking the hired car back home, it meant that Russell and I were left with no transport. Barry came to the rescue for one night, driving us both to Port Talbot where I beat Steve Newbury 3–1 and Russell lost 3–2 to Terry Griffiths, who in three years' time was to become champion of the world at the first attempt.

Barry was then called back to London on business, so Russell and I had to find our own way to Leeds by train. Leeds proved a happy hunting-ground for me. I rattled up my first century of the tour and won my match. Liverpool came next, and we were both in such cracking form that not even Ray Clemence at his best could have kept the balls out. On leaving Liverpool, the tour was over. A hectic and punishing schedule, but a golden chance to gain experience against the country's top amateurs on different tables every night and an opportunity that couldn't be equalled at this stage of my career.

As I ended up winning roughly fifty per cent of my matches, Barry was very complimentary about my performance. He had set a target on the number of matches he thought I might win, and I had lived up to his expectations.

For the rest of 1976, I remained a regular at the Lucania in Romford and received enormous encouragement from Barry, Vic, Les Coates and particularly Frank Mizzlebrook, who trapped me in corners to tell me how good I was going to be.

My biggest disappointment during early 1977 was losing 4–0 to Wally West in the English amateur, especially having beaten him so convincingly a few months earlier in the Lucania tournament.

I now realized that being expected to win put extra pressure on me. It meant I had to live up to my reputation, whereas before, as the underdog and with nothing else to lose, I had found it a lot easier to play well. This attitude of mind, of course, plays a crucial part in all forms of major competitive sport.

Undaunted by my defeat, I pushed on with great zest, and in May qualified at my third attempt for the last thirty-two of the prestigious Pontin's Open at Prestatyn. I went into the hat with eight leading professionals and drew John Pulman, world champion ten times between 1957 and 1968.

Though John was enjoying his best spell for years, I still felt I could beat him with a twenty-five start. I was in for a shock. He caned me without raising a sweat by four games to one.

We played on a poor table and I thought this would be to my advantage. But John adapted to the conditions superbly and proved that this ability to adjust to prevailing circumstances is a vital factor in a top player's armoury. These days, I'm glad to say I can usually judge a table's deficiencies after one frame.

As for the Pontin's Open, it's an annual extravaganza of snooker staged in front of a highly-knowledgeable and appreciative crowd in the vast holiday-camp complex in North Wales. Up to a thousand hopefuls join the pilgrimage to take part in a week of non-stop matches played over two frames up to the last twenty-four, at which point the professionals join in and the matches then become the best of seven.

Of course, not every day is a disaster. A notable exception was 2 August 1977. With my father watching, I achieved the ultimate in every player's snooker dream – the magical maximum break of 147 while playing Ray Martin on my home ground at the Plumstead Common Workingmen's club.

I can remember wondering for years what it would be like to make a 147, and thinking what a wonderful achievement it would be. Some days I used to pass a 147 bus on the way to Romford, and I'd wonder whether it was lucky omen.

On graduating to the 147 Club, I had made breaks of 139

and 133 the day before, so clearly I was going through the purple patch.

After potting the fifteenth black to get on the yellow, I suddenly started to quiver inside, knowing that I was so close to a 147 for the second time in a month. The previous time the maximum was in my grasp when I missed a difficult blue.

There was no problem the second time – except for a brief spell on the brown while clearing the colours. I was in a perfect position and cueing up, ready to strike, when a woman rushed past and practically knocked me off my feet in her haste to reach the toilet. I stood up, collected my composure and potted the brown, as much to my father's relief as my own. Dad said he'd have strangled her if I'd missed.

Then I banged in the blue and left myself in line on the pink. I struck it a bit too hard and instead of leaving myself a comfortable pot on the black, I left the white ball three inches from the side-cushion and dead straight. As all snooker players know, the nearer the white is to the cushion, the more difficult a shot becomes, and it's hardly the one you want when poised for your first 147.

By this time, I could hardly hold the cue. I was trembling all over. I decided that I had to hit the ball fairly hard to overcome my nerves, but as it was dead straight, I had to stun the white ball to avoid following through. In order to do this, I had to raise the butt of my cue high in the air which made the shot even more difficult. I struck the ball firmly and the black hit the near-jaw, shot across to the far-jaw, wobbled for what seemed ages, and then finally dropped in.

I remember it was a scorching hot day and the french windows were open. In a lap of honour, I walked straight out through them, came back into the club by way of the main entrance, and pushed open the snooker-room door to rapturous applause and non-stop handshaking. I telephoned Barry to break the news . . . and then played rubbish for the rest of the day.

This was one of those rare occasions when my father stopped the tuition and I packed up and celebrated with a lager too many.

A month later, with my confidence sky high, I beat Vic Harris 4–0 in the final of the Jubilee championships organized by the London and Home Counties Association. I was in one of those extra-special moods most sportsmen enjoy from time to time. I was relaxed, feeling great and bursting with enthusiasm.

My nineteenth birthday was just a week or so behind me, and I felt I had done well enough to deserve some belated presents.

Feeling in such good form, it was only natural that I was counting the days to the Lucania Pro-Am at Romford, where four top professionals – Ray Reardon, Dennis Taylor, Patsy Fagan and Doug Mountjoy – had accepted invitations to play. Lining up against them were Vic Harris, Russel Jarmak, Geoff Foulds and myself.

Romford snooker followers not only have a national reputation for providing tremendous support for their local heroes, but bet heavily among themselves. That morning was no exception. More money changed hands in the club than in Barclays across the road.

Vic was the defending champion, having beaten Alex Higgins in the final the previous year, receiving fourteen points. Geoff won the first match 3–2 in a dour struggle with Patsy Fagan, and Vic followed up with an identical victory over Doug Mountjoy in a thrilling game. Russell kept up the amateur onslaught over Dennis Taylor, and I completed the whitewash with a great 3–2 win over Reardon.

In a rest between sessions, Barry came across beaming from ear to ear and chuckling that he had placed an even-money bet on an amateur to win the title, had me at 6–1 to win the championship outright, and had backed all the amateurs individually to win their quarter-final matches.

There was nothing smooth about my progress, however,

and I gave Barry plenty of anxious heartbeats. With the game at 2–2, the final frame was a nailbiter all through.

I remember one incident vividly. Reardon snookered me cleverly on the last red and though there was a fairly simple way out, it would have meant leaving the ball in a potable position. I'd have handed him the game on a plate.

So instead of playing the straightforward shot, using one cushion, I chose to play off three, knowing that if I didn't hit the ball, at least I wouldn't present the game to him as a gift. As it was, I missed the ball by six inches.

Reardon found it impossible to restrain himself. In a voice loud enough for everyone to hear, he said, 'And he calls himself a billiards player!' He was leaving no one in doubt that he thought I had deliberately missed the ball.

For my part, I have always abided by the rules, even to the extent of admitting straightaway if the merest tip of my finger touches a ball. I made every attempt to play that ball and Reardon's reaction caused me great disappointment, because he was world champion at the time and undoubtedly the player I respected most.

The rules of snooker insist that no player shall deliberately miss. If the referee is not satisfied that a player has made a genuine attempt to strike a ball, then he has the power to make that player take the shot again from the same position.

With the four top players all beaten, Romford was instantly tagged the Graveyard of the Professionals. Except for Barry, and one or two others who had substantial bets running on the amateurs, the semi-finals were seen very much as an anti-climax – sentiments, of course, which I didn't share.

Geoff beat Vic 3–1, and I struggled to beat Russell 3–2. Considering the first frame started at 10.30 in the morning, Geoff and I were hardly fresh when we reached the table on the stroke of midnight to start the five-frame shoot-out. Going into the fourth frame, Geoff led me 2–1, but then I produced a seventy-two break at the right psychological moment both to clinch the game and put me right for the final frame.

We cued off at 1.30 in the morning and there was not a spare seat to be found in the place. A lot of large bets were still waiting to be settled. Never pressed, I won the frame comfortably. The trophy was mine, plus two hundred pounds. Yet, compared with what Barry pocketed, it was mere small change. It was the start of his policy to bet on me whenever and whoever I played.

In the 1977 Lucania championships, Barry went berserk. He bet on me in doubles and trebles and at 5–1 to win the title. After working my way through the early rounds, I reached the final – against Russell Jarmark again.

To be fair to Russell, he has plenty of ability, but just finds it impossible to believe in himself. He couldn't even believe he was in the final. He looked dreadful. He is probably the most neurotic player I have ever faced.

As usual, the championships began in a chaotic state on eight tables at 10.30 in the morning, with referees rushing around trying to bring some sanity to the scene. It turned out to be the longest tournament in which I've ever played, with the final dragging on until 4.15 the next morning.

Russell got a flyer. He won the first two frames before I bucked up and fought back to level with him. Both of us were shattered. Our eyes were closing and we were playing from memory. Neither of us really cared who won or lost. We just longed to get out of the room and home to bed.

In the final frame, Russell needed the pink and I needed both the pink and the black. After sixteen hours of non-stop snooker, that's how close and dramatic it was as we approached the climax.

I was first to play a bad safety shot. I presented Russell with a length-of-the-table chance, leaving the pink six inches from the top pocket, and the white ball just off the bottom cushion. A golden opportunity to clinch the frame, capture the trophy and send us all home to bed. It was not a certainty, but I expected him to pot it. To my surprise and delight, he missed, but the pink rolled away to safety. Twice more

I played poor safety shots, but Russell again failed to capitalize on them.

This was my first experience of playing when I was destined to win. No matter how badly I performed, Russell could not exploit my mistakes. The power of fate was dead against him.

To prove this, he missed for the third time and left the pink at my mercy. I grabbed the chance, then steadied myself for the all-important black. As soon as it dropped, I jumped up and punched the air in a victory salute which has now become a regular feature of my finale whenever I win a match that involves pressure and strain.

It's not meant to be flash or arrogant. But after all the tension a player goes through on the table, it's nice to let off steam in a big way once it's all over and you've won. In my case, I don't show much emotion when I'm playing, anyway, but that doesn't mean that it doesn't exist inside me. I'm just as human as everyone else.

As the final went on so late, some punters were worried their wives wouldn't believe they'd been at a snooker match until four in the morning, so Barry had to sign Lucania tickets to vouch for them!

With the Lucania championships under my belt, I knew that this win could, at last, act as a passport into the England amateur squad.

I also began to look and feel better. I cut my hair and had it styled. I went out and bought my first dress-suit. I began to take more interest in my appearance because I realized a good image is an important part of the act. Though I wasn't professional, I saw no harm in looking like one.

4 England Expects

Right from the start, Barry and I agreed that courtesy, politeness, smart presentation and always being on time for an appointment would help me make it to the top.

Some people might regard this theory as totally unconnected to the game of snooker, but I can assure them that I learnt very quickly that bad habits off the table have a strange knack of working their way on to the table and into a player's game.

It was while measuring for my first dress-suit that I discovered that my left arm, the one that reaches across the table, is a full two inches longer than the other. I could touch the ceiling with my left hand, but not with the right!

Obviously, I had played so much snooker during my formative years that the muscles on the left side of my body had been unusually stretched. As I'm 6 ft 2 in in height, I have a long reach anyway, but to have those extra inches as well is a definite bonus, particularly for those awkward shots when shorter players have to use the rest.

I also have double-jointed thumbs which helps to form a strong 'V' to my bridge.

On the morning after my Lucania success, Barry asked Foulds, Harris and me to join him in his office. He said he would like to arrange matches for all three of us against top players at Romford, and we jumped at the chance.

Around this time, I decided I needed to accumulate a number of trick shots to round off an evening's exhibition. I spent a few days devising a routine and a rough script of patter to go with it. The programme didn't exactly work to perfection the first time I tried it, but with constant practice it gradually improved and I realized the importance of showmanship. Since then, I have looked closely at the timing and technique used by our best comedians, and have derived a lot of benefit from seeing how they go about their work.

For the rest of 1977 I played in several small tournaments before being pitched against John Spencer, three times champion, on the match table at Romford, with him giving me fourteen points' starts.

It is no secret in business that John, like so many others, loves a bet. He once won £3,000 in a six-horse accumulator and he's not averse to backing himself if he fancies his chances at snooker.

He arrived just in time for our match, rushed into Barry's office, and asked, 'What's the betting?' 'What would you like?' Barry replied. 'It's 6–4 Steve upstairs.'

Spencer shrugged and said, 'Nonsense! I'll give you even money.'

'Why should I take even money from you when I can get 6–4 upstairs?'

'Oh, all right,' said Spencer, 'have it your own way, I'll just play.'

For fifteen minutes before the game started, a number of local bookmakers worked hard on the floor offering odds and taking a variety of bets. Barry jumped in strongly.

I played very well in the match itself, and Spencer gave me no trouble. After I'd hammered him 5–1, we shook hands and he went over to Barry and said, 'This is great. I would have lost a fortune if I'd taken your bet. As it is, I've not lost a penny, and I'm being paid my fee for playing.'

As the match finished early, Barry said to him, 'John, good luck. I've picked up a few quid, so how about playing Steve in the best of three to round off the night?'

'Certainly,' said John, 'but I'd like to pop in the Gents first.'

What followed was hilarious. A lot of the men who had backed him earlier and lost with Barry, were up on their feet and following him, like the Pied Piper, to the toilet. He was confronted on all sides by people who wanted to bet, and he had no option but to accept their challenge and bet against me beating him.

Returning to the table, he knew that only a much better performance could save him from a financial hiding. He certainly raised his concentration and played a good deal harder, but I still beat him 2–1.

With the match over, and surrounded by an army of happy punters, he turned to Barry and said, 'That's the most expensive pee I've had in my life!' Even so, he was still able to laugh at the episode, as he's one of the finest sportsmen in the game.

Since his third championship success in 1977, John has plunged down the world ratings and in 1981 was listed no higher than fifteenth. It's a sad slump because Spencer at his best is a joy to watch. He has developed a very awkward cue-action and is probably past his peak. He is far from dedicated and thinks more about playing golf and running his snooker club than he does of getting back to the top.

Motivation is vitally important. Once a player loses the will to compete, his game can collapse overnight. This happened to Spencer and is happening to others. Reardon suffered similar traumas but is trying to fight back. I dread the day when I fall in a rut and have no desire to win. This is where a good manager and good supporters play their part. They won't allow you to become complacent. Though you might not feel at your peak, they keep driving you on and won't allow you to relax.

After beating Spencer, I looked forward with relish to an important pro-am tournament at the Northern Snooker Centre. I removed a string of amateur players in the early rounds, and progressed to the quarter-finals where I received eighteen points from Ray Reardon and beat him 5–3. I also received eighteen in the semi-finals and crushed Fred Davis 5–0.

My opponent in the best-of-fifteen frame final was John Virgo, and as my father always liked to be present at a big match, he drove me up to Leeds in our shaky 1965 Mini Countryman, which clocked up thousands upon thousands of miles taking us all over England in our snooker travels.

When I walked in to face John, it seemed all Romford was there. Around forty supporters had travelled up in the early morning to make sure I received the maximum support.

To stand up in Leeds and feel you are at home in Romford is a marvellous experience. It lifted my spirits and made me even more determined to win.

When the Romford fans first arrived at the snooker centre, they clashed head-on with the Virgo supporters who had travelled from Manchester. A similar bunch of fellows who encouraged John in the same way as my supporters encouraged me.

The Romford army had pooled their money and sent Frank Mizzlebrook over to Barry with a wad of notes, urging him to find someone to take the bets. Though I was receiving ten points from John, I was still considered the outsider by both sets of fans. After an hour of wrangling, Barry finally persuaded the Virgo supporters to accept the bets and many substantial wagers were struck. Of course, I was dressing for the game in a room upstairs and it was only later that I heard how much money was put on.

My support was deafening. Probably the first time that the now famous Romford Roar was heard outside the town. Since then it has become a regular feature at all the major tournaments in which I play.

Some edgy critics complained that the roar is deliberately used to distract and unsettle my opponents. Rubbish! The vocal support is offered only at the beginning or end of a frame. As my supporters are knowledgeable snooker fans, they always pay the greatest respect to my opponents while a game is in progress. Higgins has received similar support for years, and it proves that the game is becoming more exciting. People are no longer willing just to clap their hands politely, but like to get involved and cheer their player.

I was in good form against Virgo, knocking in a break of 113 in the third frame, and from then on going from strength to strength to win the match 8–3.

There were plenty of laughs, too. I was 7–3 in front, cleaning up the colours and couldn't be caught, when Robbo, one of Romford's funniest men, stood up in the crowd, looked straight over at the deflated Virgo supporters, and holding out his hand said to them, 'Have your fares ready, gentlemen, p—lease!'

Because the tournament ended early, promoter Jim Williamson staged a best-of-three, which I won 2–1, and was rewarded with my present leather-bound cue-case.

While this tournament was taking place, I was also trying to qualify for the final of the English amateur championship. I had reached the last sixteen of the Southern Area group and, as the finals were being staged at Romford, I was expected to win.

Yet, this was one of those dreadful days when I was destined to lose. Nothing would go right for me. And with great disappointment I crashed out 4–2 to Mike Darrington in the quarter-finals.

By now I had set my heart on turning professional and I realized I had lost my gilt-edged chance of leaving the amateur ranks. I think everyone in snooker will agree that the English championship is the most difficult amateur tournament to win, probably more so in my time, because players knew that it was the only guaranteed way of becoming a professional.

There was no respite for me at that particular stage. I was chosen for England against Scotland in a friendly match held, incredibly, in the massive grandstand at Doncaster racecourse, which was far too big for a tournament that was not strictly a crowd-puller. The racecourse itself was deep under snow, and the grandstand a shivering ice-box. An unpleasant venue by any standards.

Grimsby docker Sid Hood was dropped to let me in. Announcing Hood's dismissal, the B & SCC vice-chairman, Stan Brooke, said, 'Sid's last three internationals have seen him beaten, and his form has not been what we have come to expect from him.

'At the moment, this country is rich with young talent and I believe that if we are to build a team for the future, we must look to players like Steve Davis to take on the might of Wales.'

Just to keep the peace, I beat my Scottish opponent Dave Sneddon 3-0, and England won the match with ease.

A day or so later, I was back at Romford facing Alex Higgins. I received fourteen points a frame from him, a gesture made to seem ridiculous a short time later when we faced each other as professionals.

This was definitely my toughest encounter to date. In front of a packed audience, Alex arrived an hour late, after a few problems at Ipswich, which was hardly a new experience for him as he doesn't drive.

Betting was intense. Bookmakers around the table offered me at evens, and Higgins at 4-5. The cash ran into thousands. As usual, Higgins wanted to bet on himself, and Barry accepted every penny.

The match was arranged over nine frames and, although neither of us began well, I gradually built up a three-nil lead. Then, just as the balls were being re-spotted for the fourth frame, Alex leapt to his feet and made a bee-line for Barry. He now wanted to bet himself at 8-1, confident he could fight back and win the match.

Barry burst out laughing and told him not to be so ridiculous. He told Alex he was a top-flight professional and that I was still an amateur. And that I still needed two frames to clinch the match anyway.

'All right,' said Alex, 'give me 15–2 then,' and he thrust his hand towards Barry.

Without realizing what was happening in all the noise and excitement, Barry instinctively grabbed Alex's hand and they shook on the deal. It was the most stupid bet Barry's ever made.

Alex couldn't believe his luck. Smiling his thanks, he rushed back to the table and within forty minutes had levelled the match at 3–3. Barry's heart was in his mouth, and his bicycle clips were under pressure!

The seventh frame was magic. When we came to the green, Alex showed in front by twenty points. It was my turn to play. The green was threequarters of the way down the table on the left side, between the middle hole and the black hole. Every other colour was on its spot. The white was resting just right of the yellow spot.

I got down and slammed the green into the bottom pocket and screwed back off the side cushion for the brown. The position was so perfect, the crowd went wild, cheering madly in a way that made me feel great inside. The type of roar an athlete might get if good enough to sweep past Coe in the finishing-straight.

I potted the brown, then calmly carried on to mop up the rest. Winning this game put me ahead again, and when I added the next frame as well I had triumphed 5–3.

Barry dashed over and shook my hand with such force I wondered what was so special. It was only over a curry later that night that I discovered why.

For me, the match proved the perfect preparation for my second appearance for England, this time against Wales in a home international at the luxurious Club Double Diamond in Caerphilly.

It is well known that the Welsh treat their snooker deadly seriously. It is their main indoor sport and second only to rugby overall. On one occasion, snooker even knocked the number one religion off the top. Terry Griffiths found himself Sports Personality of the Year, and rugby hero Phil Bennett, although he had just led the Lions touring team, had to settle for second place in the poll.

Producing our passports to cross the Severn Bridge, I knew we would find it tougher than St George to slay the Dragon. It seemed Wales not only had secret factories turning out brilliant half-backs like Barry John, but somewhere in the hills sudden assembly-lines were busy producing a steady flow of exceptional snooker players.

The Club Double Diamond was an excellent venue for such an important match. The place was packed out and, understandably, totally one-sided. My father, of course, travelled with me, and my mother came to watch me for the first time, along with Keith, Barry and Susan.

As a side, England were slightly weaker than the Welsh. We knew early on that a struggle was on the cards. Thankfully, I justified my selection by beating John Prosser 2–1, but the night was best remembered for the wonderful Welsh welcome we received, and for a spectacular fall by Jerry Lambert, then president of the London Home Counties Association.

Jerry was sitting on the top row of a line of tiered seating, about four feet from the floor, enjoying the after-match cabaret. One joke tickled him so much, he rocked violently on his chair, tipped backwards and crashed to the ground – still holding his pint of lager!

Next morning, unhurt and without a bruise, Jerry insisted that he was so drunk when he hit the ground that he felt nothing. I can remember the moment we all rushed up to him, and all he cared about was whether he'd lost any lager.

By now the Pontin's tournament had come round again, and I slowly picked my way through the qualifying rounds until I reached the last thirty-two. There I faced Tony Knowles, later to turn professional. I lost the first two frames, but managed to claw back to 3–3. The crunch came with me needing the last red and black, plus all the colours up to the pink, to win the match.

I potted the red and black, but played a poor positional shot which left me cueing over the green, six inches away from the cushion just past the middle pocket towards the top cushion. To pot the yellow on its own would not have been too difficult. But, as I needed to screw back a long way to get position on the green, it made the pot ten times harder.

As it turned out, it was probably the best shot I have ever played. I raised my butt well into the air to dig down into the white ball in order to screw back, and powered the yellow home. I couldn't have expected the pot to go any more perfectly. I screwed back a full seven feet to leave myself an easy position to clear the colours. Tony was sick. To get position on the green seemed impossible.

I progressed through the following rounds, beat Reardon in the semis and came up against Tony Meo in the final. And what a final! The crowd appreciated it so much they all stood up and cheered us at the end for a full five minutes. I have the last six frames on video, and people still come up to me and say it was the best match they've ever seen.

Tony won the first two frames, but once I had clicked into gear we reached the interval with me showing ahead 4–2. I won the first frame of the evening session, but Tony then enjoyed one of his sparkling spells and put together two splendid breaks of ninety-seven and seventy-two, and led me 6–5.

The twelfth frame was yet another nailbiter. Tony had a superb chance to clinch the match on the brown, but missed. He left me on, and I cleaned up to level the match at 6–6. So came the deciding thirteenth frame. I drew first blood with a twenty and, after a few safety shots, he left me up again and I compiled a match-winning break of fifty-six, all consisting of pinks. It was one of the most important breaks of my life.

This win earned me a handsome £1,500 in cash and a Pontinental holiday. Before going into the final, Tony and I had agreed that we would split the prize-money. I was more interested in the title! Nevertheless, I now know that it was a wrong decision. It was not professional. Barry and I discussed it later and agreed that in future I would never split prize-money for any tournament.

5 The Large Pond

Shortly after that Pontin's triumph, Barry decided that instead of just practising through the summer, I should tour his twenty Lucania clubs, meeting members and playing those who fancied their chances against me.

Most of the clubs were in or near London. Because I had to travel by bus, Barry lent me a Maxi. It was my first car and, though not strictly my own, I found it a great thrill to be able to go from place to place with such independence.

My confidence soared after winning the Pontin's Open, and although Tony Knowles beat me the following week in the Warner's Open, I longed to challenge professionals on level terms.

My wish was granted when Doug Mountjoy played me at Romford and beat me 5-2, underlining in no uncertain terms that I still had a long way to go. A month after playing Doug I met Patsy Fagan in a similar challenge match, and this time made no mistake, winning 5-1.

Playing professionals in this way obviously appealed to my ego much more than competing against amateurs, although I was sensible enough to understand that until I actually established myself as a top amateur I would not be in a position to turn professional. Financially I couldn't complain, because all restrictions on prize money had been scrapped, allowing me to pocket several big cash prizes.

The CIU national championships were considered a prestige amateur event, and in early July I reached the semi-final against the popular Welshman Alwyn Lloyd, an excellent player who received strong support no matter where he played.

We met at Coventry, and Barry burst into the room and told the Welsh people he fancied a bet. The Welsh immediately huddled in a scrum, from which their spokesman broke away and asked Barry how much he had in mind.

'Leave it to you,' said Barry.

'All right,' came the reply, 'ten, ten, ten . . . five tens!' At least that's what he thought he heard.

Barry then confirmed that all bets were on, but asked them why no one had risked a decent one.

'Decent bet, man?' came the reply. 'You've already got five hundred quid from us. How much more do you want?'

Barry was baffled. Then it dawned on him. The Welshman hadn't said 'ten' at all. He had said 'ton'.

Both sides eventually settled on five separate bets of fifty pounds, and the Welsh went to their pews smiling contentedly. They were happier when Alwyn took the first two frames, and you could practically hear them lubricating their vocal chords over at the bar.

Not for long, though. I eventually found my rhythm, achieved some of my best snooker and won the next two frames to draw level. The choir had been silenced.

The third frame was a humdinger. Brown, blue, pink and black were left on the table, and I required the blue to win. In potting the brown, I had no alternative but to leave my white in the jaws of the bottom left-hand pocket. With the blue on its spot, it meant I had a virtually dead-straight chance of potting it into the top right-hand pocket.

I considered playing a safety shot, but decided in the end to go for the blue, and cued it perfectly. I accepted that the blue wasn't a good percentage shot, but something odd inside me pushed me on to attack the ball in that way. Such a feeling comes over me a lot in snooker and when it does, I usually find that if I go for my shot, it pays off.

It did this time, and it was the turn of my supporters to raise the roof. This, of course, put me 3–2 in front, and the next frame saw me over the line.

To give the Welsh lads credit, they remained in the club for a long night of celebrations, and entertained the London crowd with some wonderful singing, especially from Alwyn. This put pressure on me to get up and sing, but I had to decline because even my rubber duck cringes at the sound of my voice.

Birmingham's dour Jack Fitzmaurice was my opponent in the final. A player with tons of tenacity and a man who must never be underestimated. Jack had been around a long time, and some years earlier had finished runner-up in the All-England championships.

Again we played in Coventry, and again the club was jam-packed. One of our lads complained it was so hot in the room that the sweat ran down his nose and into his beer.

Barry arrived like a guard from Securicor. He had never carried so much cash in one day. He was certain I would win and went around the room pleading for people to bet. But no one wanted to know. Just like him, they all thought I was a good thing.

Although I am regularly surrounded by people like Barry who love to invest on my chances, betting on myself is something that has never appealed to me. To this day, I have never put a penny on myself in any type of tournament. I believe there is enough to think about in a game without pushing the pressure up even higher by worrying over the consequences of a losing bet.

Barry's disappointment at not obtaining a bet at Coventry was hardly eased when I shot into a three-nil lead. Jack then pulled one back, and in the fifth frame he held an unassailable forty-point lead when we came to the pink.

Feeling that I had lost my edge, and that Jack was in overdrive, I decided to keep the pink on the table for as long as I could and try for snookers. I didn't expect to win the frame, but thought it might upset Jack's rhythm.

Although I never knew whether it was these tactics which actually did it, I recovered to win the next frame, clinch the match by four games to two, and go away with the CIU title.

At the same time as winning that snooker championship, I was qualifying for the final of the CIU billiards final, and hoping to complete a unique and important double. But if you've heard of the name Norman Dagley, then you'll realize the remote type of chance I had. Norman had been world amateur billiards champion on more than one occasion. Second place was a certainty even before I took my cue from its case.

Still, I was the first player for thirty years to reach both finals at the same time, and I felt satisfied that this achievement was enough in itself and augured well for the future.

Winning the CIU snooker title not only gave me a valid reason to celebrate, but also meant that I had now possibly accomplished enough as an amateur to turn professional. Barry and I decided that if I was going to continue to improve at the same rate, I should join the professionals and become a small fish in a large pond and hopefully, before long, a piranha!

I applied for professional status a short time later and asked whether, if I were accepted, my registration could be deferred until 17 September, so that I could continue to fulfil my obligations as an amateur. One of these was the national team championships in which Geoff Foulds, Vic Harris and I strolled away with the title at the Commonwealth Sporting Club, Blackpool.

Barry submitted the application form on my behalf, and on 4 June 1978 I signed a five-year contract appointing him as my manager. It was the typical one-sided contract. We copied it from one used by a snooker agency, removed the names and typed in our own.

The contract stipulated that I would do everything Barry instructed, that I wouldn't act without consulting him first, and that I'd agree to him taking ten per cent of everything I earned. Actually, we never once looked at that contract again, let alone stuck by it. I still haven't worked out why we needed that piece of paper in the first place.

In the beginning, a player could just declare himself a professional and he was in. That was a stupid situation, which disappeared when the World Professional Billiards and Snooker Association was formed to keep the best players together.

Barry immediately set about building up my public image. He called a Press conference and told reporters, 'It won't be long now before he turns pro. Already none of the élite want to play him. He is good enough to show them up and is making more money than a lot of the lesser professionals.

'He doesn't drink, smoke or gamble. He's single-minded. His relaxation is playing mental chess. No board. No pieces. Everything in his head. He's the most dedicated professional you could hope to meet. He's a certainty.

This, of course, was nothing more than a shrewd public relations exercise. A job which Barry loves, and one which he performs better than anyone I know. For me, the excitement was tremendous. It was a big step to take and I felt very pleased with myself.

My first opportunity to play abroad came in August 1978. Lucania Snooker Clubs agreed to pay my expenses to fly off and challenge the world's top professionals in the Canadian Open, spanning two weeks in the busy city of Toronto. Even though it was an Open competition, the amateurs were still expected to play on level terms with the professionals, so it was yet another extreme test of my technique and temperament.

I disposed of several useful Canadians early on, plus Willie Thorne, a good English professional who, I am sure, would do so much better if he began to believe in himself and his potential. Eventually I reached the quarter-finals, where I faced none other than Alex Higgins.

Described by the Press as a 'classic of its kind', the match eventually went to Higgins by nine games to eight. Considering we played off levels, I felt I had shown the snooker world my improvement. Like the Press, I also regarded it as one of my best matches. But for my slight lack of experience, I might have won.

Being knocked out meant I had a few days in which to tour the country, and I made a point of grabbing the chance to see the breathtaking Niagara Falls at first hand. It certainly lived up to its reputation.

I arrived home on 13 September, and a few days later it was back to work. I went straight into the Lucania Masters, a new knockout competition made up of sixteen of the country's top amateurs, played at Romford for a first prize of five hundred pounds. It was hardly a happy return for me because Cliff Wilson, that amusing, genial Welshman, struck peak form and beat me 3–2 in the final after I had stupidly gone in off the green, attempting a safety shot in the deciding frame.

A month later Cliff went to Malta, where he won the world amateur championship, and turned professional immediately on his return.

Cliff is a fine attacking player, extremely dangerous in a short game, and someone who probably turned professional about twenty years too late. He is too adventurous to win a major competition, but in his early years he definitely put some mystic spell on Ray Reardon, who found it terribly hard to beat him.

The following weekend I retained the Lucania Pro-Am title, beating Vic Harris 5–1 in the final. Vic joked that if the match had gone its distance I would have had to concede the professionals' obligatory fourteen-point start. I cracked back that that was why I finished the match off before midnight – when I officially became a professional.

My entry into the pro ranks was marked by a small party. Barry and Susan joined my mum, dad, Keith and me for a celebratory Indian meal and a few bottles of white wine.

Now that I had joined the professionals, Barry decided that

Reardon should be invited back to Romford to play me in a 27-frame match stretching over two days.

I welcomed the opportunity to meet Reardon in these circumstances, because I could use him as a yardstick on which to measure my own improvement. I beat him 14–11, and on leaving the room after the game, I was asked by one of the Romford lads if I had enjoyed playing Reardon. I remember telling him, 'Definitely. I'm drinking his blood.'

On reflection this seemed appropriate, as some players have nicknamed him Count Dracula. I don't think he minds greatly because it tends to suggest considerable strength of character.

I felt I could learn more from playing Reardon than from any other professional in the game. My career had reached the stage where I had to learn more. Not just the basic techniques, but all the various ploys and subtle tactics used by the professionals.

Almost immediately I noticed that the big difference between the amateur and professional was the way in which chances were taken when they came along. As an amateur, it seemed I had three chances to win a frame. As a professional, there was just about one. I began to appreciate the value of capitalizing on other people's mistakes.

In ninety-five per cent of all frames in top-class snooker, both players in a game get one definite chance to take command and win the game. It's the players who make the most of these opportunities who are the more successful. This is where consistency plays such a vital part, and is one of the main points my father and I always concentrated on. Early on as a professional, I realized it was not so much my best performance that mattered, as my worst.

In my match against Reardon, I had no doubt he was trying as hard at the end as he was at the beginning. My victory captured a great deal of attention in the newspapers, and this probably helped to push my claim for a place on BBC's popular Pot Black series, although I firmly believe the main reason was that I was a new professional and my name was Davis!

Quite a stir blew up when the BBC announced that I had been selected and that Higgins had been dropped. To me, it seemed fairly obvious that Higgins had been penalized for his bad behaviour in the previous year's competition.

I shall never forget my introduction to Pot Black, mainly because it was my first major competition in which most of the senior professionals took part. The excitement was electrifying, and something I had never experienced before.

I was as nervous as a kitten in the days leading up to the competition. As Pot Black is always recorded between Christmas and the New Year, my seasonal celebrations were cut to half a glass of lager and the occasional cheese roll while I put in many hours of solo practice.

Before playing in my first game I went for a meal in the hospitality room at the Pebble Mill studio in Birmingham, where the series is recorded. By some strange coincidence, my first match involved none other than my namesake Fred Davis – the young versus the old!

As I entered the room, the first person I saw was the ever-smiling, ever-affable Fred. I sat opposite him at the same table and as I was about to tuck into my meal, I noticed a curious glint in his eye. He said to me, 'Steve, you're not having the pork are you?'

'Yes,' I said. 'Why?'

The glint grew, and back came the reply, 'Oh, brother Joe always used to say you can't pot a ball after eating pork.'

I burst out laughing and told Fred he would need to do better than that if he wished to wind me up before a game.

After the first few shots, all the tension that had built up inside me during the previous week faded swiftly and I got down to the job in hand. One shot I remember in particular, especially for the commentary by Ted Lowe, involved me potting a tremendous long red down the left-hand side cushion into the top pocket. I've watched the shot several times on the

video since, and it never fails to raise a smile as Ted says
'... and I think Steve will be playing a thin safety shot with
a little left-hand side to bring the white ball back nicely down
the – Goodness me, he's potted it!'

Gradually I pulled away from Fred, and by the colours I
was safely home – pork or no pork! To the time of writing this
book, I have not won another frame on Pot Black, and I can
assure everyone that it has absolutely nothing to do with what
I eat in the hours leading up to the matches.

Most professionals prefer to play in long matches, and find
the one-frame, sudden-death demands of Pot Black unappeal-
ing. Yet, though it is little more than a high-class lottery, Pot
Black has played a prominent part in making the game so
immensely popular with the general public.

After beating Fred, my next frame threw me into combat
with Doug Mountjoy. A win would have guaranteed me a
place in the semi-finals, but after going in–off, Doug produced
an eighty-two break from nowhere and I needed to beat Perrie
Mans by at least twenty-five points to stay in the competition.
I failed and that was the end of my initial taste of Pot Black.

My first confrontation with Cliff Thorburn came in the
Castle Pro-Am in Southampton, exactly a week after my exit
from Pot Black. Since arriving from Canada in 1973, Thorburn had acquired an international reputation as being the
hardest man in the game. Someone who relished nothing more
than to see his opponents screwed into the ground.

Thankfully, there was no sign of this pressure-building as
our match got under way. I coasted into a three-frame lead
with incredible ease. Then someone, somewhere, must have
remembered to flick the switch. Suddenly, the docile Canadian turned from being a struggling loser into a stampeding
attacker with a hard-bitten face. Full of that aggressive
purpose I had heard so much about. During the next four
frames I hardly saw a ball, and he powered off with the match
by four games to three, leaving me wondering where I had
gone wrong.

Just to break things up slightly, I then entered the UK Crystalite billiards championships, reaching the quarter-final only to come face to face with the inimitable John Barrie. Few people know that John's real name is Barrie Smith, but because at least three other Smiths were doing so well at billiards when he started, he was advised to change his name by Joe Davis, who rated him a great prospect and gave him every encouragement.

Acknowledged by the other players as the expert on top-of-the-table play, and probably the only man capable of making a thousand break at billiards, John inflicted the most terrible hammering on me. In between the breaks of four hundred and two hundred, I remembered squeezing in a devastating two, and sitting down again wondering what I was doing there.

I went away earning a hundred pounds – gross over-payment considering the score-line. To make the day worse, I discovered that not only did my billiards need some brushing up, but my angles with the birds weren't very clever either. I met one at the hotel and she got so bored she fell asleep on me!

Leaving aside Pot Black, my first real experience of professional tournament snooker came at the Corn Exchange in Ipswich. Along with Higgins, Reardon and Mountjoy, I was invited to play in the Tolly Cobbold championships, decided on a round-robin basis.

I beat Higgins 4–0 in my first match, and then quickly went two up against Mountjoy, only to draw 2–2. On seeing the results in the other groups, I knew I needed just one frame from four against Reardon to clinch my place in the final.

When Reardon and I walked in, you could practically touch the tension. Reardon won the first two frames, mainly through taking advantage of some unforced errors of mine. I realized later I was in the wrong frame of mind. Instead of looking to win the match as a whole, I was concerned only with capturing the single frame I needed.

Then came the rumpus. As the referee set the balls up for

the third frame, Reardon complained that the reds had not been placed correctly. He said he would not break off until they were reset. The referee politely did as he asked.

'Still not right,' said Reardon. So the referee started all over again.

By now, the referee was in such a flap that when he placed the reds for the third time, the first thing he did was to look over at Reardon, simply begging him to say 'yes'. But Reardon remained stubbornly unmoved and shook his head. For some reason, known only to himself, he was making a major issue out of absolutely nothing.

On six occasions Reardon made the referee reset those balls, most of the time delivering his instructions from his 'vantage' point way back beyond the baulk!

Of course, the referee should have used his authority and ordered Reardon to play on or lose the frame. This is why all top referees should be of strong character and be seen to be in control of the game.

During the long hold-up, I became very embarrassed. I just stood around like a lemon. When we eventually got back to the game, my concentration was in tatters. Apart from a remote chance in the fourth frame, which I fluffed, all my hopes of winning the match had gone, and Reardon beat me 4-0.

It was only when I returned to the cool of my dressing-room that I fully appreciated what had gone on. This bout of gamesmanship was obviously designed to unsettle me. I was annoyed with Reardon at the time, although, as it turned out, he had taught me a lesson. I realized I had made an elementary mistake by remaining in the room while the trouble brewed. Of course, I should have turned round and walked out. Furious for not realizing this in the hall, I vowed never to put myself in such an embarrassing position again.

In the end, I emerged from the Ipswich fiasco in third place, having won an exciting play-off with Mountjoy, after Higgins had beaten Reardon in a gripping final. Third place might not have been as good as first, but I was satisfied at least that I had gone down well in Ipswich.

On my first visit to Pontin's in May 1975, when dad and I saw Reardon in close up for the first time, we quickly realized why he was world champion – the Jack Nicklaus of the 1970s.

He possessed an air of superiority that probably unsettled a few players. He was a shrewd tactician and the most consistent player around. I remember thinking that of all the players in the game, he was the one I most wanted to emulate.

As time went by, and I started to play him, I realized just how tough an opponent he could be. As an ex-policeman Reardon doesn't yield easily. You have to go on hitting him hard with your truncheon before he finally submits!

In recent times, I have noticed a definite slide in him. He is no longer the force he was during his impressive reign as champion. My only serious criticism of his game concerns the habit he has of lifting his head on a shot, especially for a screwback. Though this never seemed to affect his play in his heyday, such bad habits now appear to be letting him down when things aren't going so well for him. In spite of all this, I must say I have learnt a lot from Ray Reardon, in particular the importance of the final backswing, which few professionals incorporate in their play. In addition to all the skills he had displayed on the table, Reardon has also proved to be an excellent ambassador for the game.

Shutting the Reardon defeat out of my mind, I went straight to Manchester to play John Virgo in the final of the Demmy Pro-Am. Having beaten John in the Northern Snooker Centre final when receiving ten, I felt my game had improved so much since then, that I could cope with him off levels, even allowing for the match being played on his home table.

What a shock I had in store. He murdered me 5–0. Yet in every frame we played, I always had a good chance, but it was one of those nights when nothing went right.

John is a strange mixture of moods. One minute he can be

the funniest man on earth, and the next miserably deep and withdrawn.

On one of my rare days off, I visited Cheltenham races to present the trophy to the winner of the Coral Golden Hurdle. Several snooker players were there, including John, a great lover of the Turf, and true to form he became increasingly quiet as the day went by.

He had no luck with his bets, and as his horses lost one by one, his eyes showed more and more dejection. It was only when his horse in the last race crossed the line in front that he let out a loud 'Come on, my son' and his eyes sparkled again and he returned to his normal self.

To John's credit, he is not frightened to speak his mind, though this has been known to upset one or two people from time to time. There was a spell, too, when he was not the game's best loser, but he's improved a lot in this respect.

He hasn't enjoyed the best of luck in televised tournaments either. When he won the Corals United Kingdom championships in 1979 the technicians were out on strike. A big coverage then would have done his image – and his diary – a power of good.

John's personality doesn't project itself on the table, and it's surprising the number of people who think he is a nasty character. Hopefully for John his television debut in the 1981 world championships as a talented impersonator of other players has corrected this entirely wrong impression.

One thing is sure, John doesn't lack skill. He is undoubtedly one of the cleverest break-builders in the game.

My next engagement was, in the words of Monty Python, 'something completely different' when Barry arranged a marathon 65-frame match for me against Alex Higgins at Romford. It stretched over four days and attracted capacity crowds and, even more important, considerable Press coverage.

For six of the eight sessions, Higgins was unbelievably well behaved. Almost a gentleman. Then he cracked. The seeds of trouble were planted as early as the first morning, before the match had even started. Higgins was so confident he would beat me that he went off and put a lot of money on himself. What he didn't take into account was that I knew the table inside out and that he was stepping into a minefield.

I eventually beat him thirty-three frames to twenty-three, although he first conceded at the end of the sixth session when the score was 31–18. He simply turned to the crowd and told them not to come back next day because he wouldn't be there. Then he charged down to Barry's office on the ground floor and shouted at everyone in sight. Barry led him off into a private room and told him he could leave at that moment and that a new player would be found to take his place.

When he stormed out, we thought that was the last we'd see of him. But Alex is such an unpredictable Jekyll and Hyde character that you never know what he's going to do next. This was no exception. When we turned up next morning, who should be there but Alex, apologizing profusely for everything that had happened the day before and raring to do his best on the table.

He was in scintillating form and gave the crowd a delightful exhibition of exciting snooker. Though I won the first frame, he won the next five in a row before I wrapped it all up 33–23.

In a match of unsurpassable snooker, Alex produced breaks of 132, 93, 80, 75, 73, 59 and 53. Not to be outdone, I knocked in 132, 102, 87, 82, 81, 73, 72, 71, 66, 64, 64 and 54. And in all the other frames, there was never a break of less than 40.

All those people lucky enough to see the match had more than value for money. More important, from my point of view, I found I could stay the distance. And at no time was I ruffled or disturbed by the Higgins antics.

Alex is definitely a man of two minds. On the one side, he can be totally obnoxious, while on the other hand he can be quite charming. Love him or hate him, he has tremendous charisma, and no player in the world can argue that he hasn't been good for the game. I believe his conduct often depends on the amount of drink he has inside him. More important, I believe he likes to be the centre of attention all the time and when this is taken away from him, he airs his frustrations.

By the 1981 world championships, Alex's steady decline was being noticed for the first time. He was irritable because he could no longer achieve what he used to attain. If he is to remain a powerful force in the game and recapture his full range of shots, I think he will have to take an urgent and hard look at himself.

6 Snow Strands 'Iceman'

With my name now in the newspapers a lot more often and the
game receiving considerable coverage on television, the Coral
bookmaking organization, ever alert to new opportunities,
started to take a personal interest in me and in snooker in
general.

Their marketing manager, David Brimacombe, suggested
that his company should organize a nationwide tour of fifteen
matches that would involve nightly confrontations between
me and the Coral United Kingdom champion, Doug Mountjoy.

Corals offered us both £2,000 which was good money for
me at the time. I was happy with the contract, and signed
straightaway. Doug, however, was not so excited. As United
Kingdom champion, he thought he should receive more than
me. Corals didn't agree and Doug withdrew. I must say I
thought he had a point. Determined to push on with their
plans, Corals signed up Fred Davis, and the tour finally got
under way in March.

Midway through the series the weather turned foul. We had
played at Newcastle and our next stop was Middlesbrough.
During the night a blizzard swept the north-east, and the AA
warned that roads were impassable. I had arranged to meet
a girl in Middlesbrough and she must have been a bit special
because against all the odds and common sense, I set off to try
to complete the forty miles and keep the date.

Travelling farther south, the snow became even heavier,
and the traffic noticeably less by the minute. Cars and lorries

were abandoned in all places and at all angles. It was like a bobsleigh run.

Over the radio, the AA reported that the A I was blocked near Darlington and advised all drivers daft enough to still be on it to find an exit or leave their vehicles where they were and walk to safety. Already fifteen hundred cars and lorries were reported abandoned on the A I alone.

Thinking the serious drifts were a lot farther south, I turned off for Middlesbrough. Front-wheel drive on the Maxi enabled me to travel a lot farther than most other motorists and I really believed I had cut through the Arctic conditions.

Then out of the blue a six-foot wall of snow loomed up in front of me and I came to a halt just like the rest. I panicked. I was freezing in the middle of nowhere with snow stacked high around me and no sign of life. I tried to reverse, but to no avail. I was stuck. All of a sudden I felt really frightened.

'Thank God,' I thought, as a man with a suitcase came around the drift on his way to the small town of Sedgefield and said stranded motorists were being served there with tea and sandwiches.

I grabbed my cue and my case and followed him through the snow, knee deep at times to this little oasis in the back of beyond. It was so bitterly cold I pulled on two pairs of socks as gloves to carry my bags.

On reaching the town hall, and gulping a hot drink, my main concern was to find a telephone to tell people of my predicament. Eventually, I found the phone – and twenty other people queuing up to use it. By the time my turn came round, the coin-box was full and it seized up. I was now well and truly cut off from the living world. However, a couple in the hall called Roger and Jackie Place kindly said I could borrow their telephone at home and told me I could sleep in their spare room until the roads were opened.

Back at Newcastle, it was obvious to Fred that conditions were deteriorating. I telephoned his hotel, only to find he had

been whisked off to some nice warm radio station to appear on
a phone-in programme.

Two days went by before the weather finally relented
enough for me to go looking for the Maxi. Even then my
troubles were far from over. On reaching the car I found the
snow still up to the bonnet, the driver's door prized open and
my radio ripped out.

Wrapped up against the wind, I borrowed a shovel and
began to dig an escape route, thinking all the time whether I
should be risking an injury with the world championships just
a month away.

With two days knocked out of our programme, it meant
Fred and I had to miss our matches in Middlesbrough and
Sheffield.

Corals arranged the tour in such a way that we each played
the best of three frames against an amateur nominated by the
club we were visiting. If an amateur won a match, he received
a hundred pounds in free bets from Corals. If he won a single
frame, he received twenty-five pounds in free bets. Somehow
I succeeded in going through the tour without losing a match,
although Fred, in a very relaxed mood, did lose one.

The tour's last match was booked for the Lucania at
Romford. It was decided to split the day, Fred and I playing
the amateurs in the afternoon, and the two of us playing each
other in a charity match over nine frames in the evening for
the Joe Davis Memorial Trophy. Joe's widow, June, gave
permission for us to use the great man's name, provided all
proceeds went to Cancer Research.

First, the amateurs had to be faced, and I, more than
anyone else, realized that Romford's reputation as the graveyard of the professionals was about to be tested yet again. Up
to this point, as many as thirteen professionals had played
there and an amateur had won every time. Now for a change,
I was returning as a professional and determined to end the
long and embarrassing sequence.

Alas, Tony Putnam, a good, young prospect, maintained

the remarkable jinx, and beat me 2–0. What's more, Fred did only marginally better, losing 2–1 to Vic Harris. Corals, I am certain, thought the whole affair was a fix, which gave me even more reason to feel annoyed with myself. My form was not much better in the evening, Fred beating me by five frames to three. I left the table thinking it might have been better if I had stayed in bed that day.

Fred's knowledge of the game is immense, and the experience I gained on that tour with him couldn't have been found elsewhere. Admittedly his potting was starting to wane, but the chance to be in his company night after night, studying his technique, all helped to broaden my view of the game.

Fred reached the semi-finals of the 1978 world championships at the age of sixty-four, an absolutely tremendous feat and one which emphasizes that there is no substitute for experience. Fred smiles a lot, but behind that smile is one of the hardest players the game has ever known. It has been said that even if he were kicking you in the teeth, Fred would be sure to do it with a smile.

With the tour over, all attention was turned to the 1979 world championships. This was my first opportunity to reach out for the ultimate prize in our wonderful game, and a chance to join the list of the all-time greats. There is no higher pinnacle than being champion of the world. I believe it should be every player's prime objective. It's everything we work for, practise for and pray for.

The draw pitched me against Ian Anderson, an Australian, in the first qualifying round at Leeds, with the winner to play Patsy Fagan at Stockport for the right to go on to the competition proper at The Crucible Theatre in Sheffield, the undisputed mecca of the sport.

Barry was bursting with optimism. He was confident I would reach Sheffield. One bookmaker offered him 2–1 on my qualifying and he snapped it up. All my faithful followers flocked to Leeds and though Anderson took one frame on the black, I put together a string of big breaks and thrashed him 9-1.

So on I went to Stockport, still accompanied by my loyal and lively entourage.

Patsy Fagan was suffering from all sorts of problems. At his peak, he was a great amateur, a marvellous money player and red-hot at cleaning up the colours. His troubles began shortly after winning the 1977 United Kingdom championships. He was booked for exhibitions at the Warner's holiday camps, but was involved in a bad car accident, wrenching the muscles in his right arm. This crash shook him terribly and it might have caused him to step up too much on his drinking.

The story goes that his game first cracked when he missed a vital pink using the rest in the 1978 world championships against Fred Davis. From then on, Patsy developed a dreadful phobia for the rest. Try as he did, he found it extremely difficult to recapture his confidence with it, and only now has he recovered, although he's still not back to his best. I can only imagine it's like someone losing his confidence on the top diving board, and freezing at the sight of people waiting for him to plunge.

Ironically, Patsy was one of the best pressure players in the game. On numerous occasions against me, and others, he has won frames from impossible positions by cleaning up the last reds and the colours. Being unable to play a shot with the rest inevitably upset him so much that it became embarrassing for him. He even consulted a hypnotist for help. Sadly, this failed, too, and he had to wait until his confidence and assurance returned to him naturally.

Curiously, I was introduced as the 'iceman' of snooker for our match, the compliment that had always been associated with Patsy. To be honest, I was trembling like a rabbit and in serious need of Barry's bicycle clips.

Even though Patsy had shown improved confidence with the rest leading up to these world championships, he was clearly still having enormous problems with it. I decided that whenever possible I would try not to watch him playing his shots, thinking they might affect me the same way. I was definitely not at my best with the rest that day. As expected, Patsy was far from being in top nick, and I was not pressed to beat him 9–3.

Whenever required to use the rest as a youngster, I never dodged it. I never climbed on to the table or overstretched. As a result, I now find that I have mastered it to such an extent that I can even play power shots with it. Success or failure with the rest depends entirely on a player's attitude. At no time should he be frightened of it. He must always show a firm and positive approach. One player who admits to not liking the rest is Dennis Taylor who sometimes tries to overcome the problem by swopping hands for the shot – much, I should imagine, to the horror of his supporters.

The dream of playing at The Crucible was suddenly a reality. I could now truly say that I had arrived in the big time. Yet, 'iceman' or not, I became pretty stirred up over it. I knew the draw, the players involved, and the television coverage. The only thing I didn't know about was the atmosphere in the theatre itself, and the effect it would have on me while walking out to face a thousand staring faces and millions more on TV.

As Dennis Taylor is probably the most humorous of all the snooker players, a lot of leg-pulling was guaranteed before we faced each other in the first round proper. Dennis wasted no time in launching into the wisecracks. When I asked him if Patricia planned to come up for the game, he simply said, 'No, not this one. She's just coming up for the final.'

You can never be offended by anything Dennis says. He loves to wind people up. And he is an expert at exchanging banter with hecklers in the crowd. His wit and skill make him very popular at the clubs, where he is in constant demand for exhibition matches between tournament appearances. Dennis is never nasty, never malicious and he is a great sport.

Our match was tight from the start. I opened up with a fifty-seven, though the balls were so well placed, I should have made a hundred. I lost position slightly and was forced to play from near a cushion and missed. To my horror, Dennis stepped in and mopped up with a sixty-one.

Every single point was hard-earned by both of us. We ground on from 2–2 to 7–7 before Dennis pulled away to 9–7 and eventually to 12–9, needing just one more frame for the match.

At this point, Dennis might have thought he had done enough to win, but I pulled myself together and managed to close the gap to 12–11. Dennis had suddenly lost his rhythm and with the reds wide open, all I needed was a long blue into the top corner pocket to put me among them. Call it pressure, call it inexperience – but I missed it. From that moment, Dennis regained control and won the match 13–11.

I felt I had coped well with the pressure surrounding my first visit to The Crucible, although I never produced anything exceptional.

More than anything else, I discovered the atmosphere of the world championships have no parallel anywhere else in the game. The drama and tension are completely exclusive to this incomparable tournament. In 1981, Dave Martin was so worked up in his dressing-room that he was physically sick just fifteen minutes before going out to play Bill Werbeniuk. And I remember finding it hard going with my smoked haddock at breakfast before playing Dennis Taylor.

As for the television coverage, I was disappointed. Just twenty minutes of the match were shown, and almost all the time was devoted to Dennis scoring the only century break of the game. Shots of me were confined to my occasional miss and to the one when I potted the white directly into the top pocket. For the next month, people kept telling me that I didn't play very well, which brought home to me the power and influence that television has on us all.

Press coverage was just a little better, with some newspapers claiming that I had made history of some sort by becoming the only player ever to eat a ham sandwich during the world championships while his match was still in progress. Having only picked at my haddock, I was absolutely starving when the morning session stretched into the afternoon. I had gone five hours without a meal, and with still another frame to play, I asked a steward to bring me something to keep me going. Many people didn't like what they saw and complained that I was giving the game a bad image. Looking back, it probably wasn't the right thing to do, but I was so hungry I felt it was affecting my game.

Just as he predicted and, in my opinion, playing the best snooker of his life, Dennis swept on to the final, beating Ray Reardon at the quarter stage and John Virgo in the semis. Only newcomer Terry Griffiths stood between him and his finest hour.

Like me, it was Terry's first visit to The Crucible and only his second season as a professional. He was invincible that year, making a mockery of those bookmakers who rated him no better than a 33–1 chance. He literally turned from being a part-time insurance agent to a world champion overnight.

Showing amazing coolness, he squeezed past Higgins and Charlton, produced the goods when required and was a thoroughly worthy champion. One of Terry's strongest points is his long potting, and it was devastating that year. He has a huge range of shots, and you would have to go a long way to find a better player with the rest.

7 Bringing the House Down

Straight after the pressure and excitement of the world championships came the most enjoyable week of the snooker year – especially for the professionals, who had the chance to wind down mentally.

In all my previous visits to Pontin's, I had always played as an amateur, receiving a big start whenever meeting a professional. Now, for the first time, I was taking part as one of the eight invited professionals, along with Reardon, Spencer, Charlton, Mountjoy, Mans, Miles and Fred Davis.

For the first time at Pontin's, I had to give starts instead of receiving them.

As usual, the professionals were introduced to the holiday-makers on the Sunday night and when asked whether I hoped to capture the professional tournament, I jokingly said, 'Yes – and I'm out to retain my Open title, as well!'

Alas, Graham Miles played brilliantly to beat me 4–0, and I assumed my involvement for that year was well and truly over. Graham is probably one of the most inconsistent of all the professionals. At his best, he is a smooth, classy cueist; at his worst, he looks incapable of potting a ball. This I put down entirely to his unorthodox action, in which the cue runs almost in line with his left ear.

I never expected to achieve much in the pro-am event, but after some hard battles, I found myself in the semi-final against John Spencer. I beat him 4–0 to earn myself a title chance against Jimmy White, the youngest-ever English amateur champion. And I had to give him thirty start!

Steve Davis has arrived.
His first photo session

Steve Davis
wins the
1980 Coral
UK Snooker
Championship

Steve Davis with
Tony Meo in the
final of the 1981
John Courage
English Snooker
Championship

Steve Davis with his
parents, Bill and Jean

Steve Davis beat Terry Griffiths in the second round of the 1980
World Championship

Steve Davis with Alex Higgins before the second round of the 1981
World Championship

A tense moment for
Alex Higgins in the
World
Championship,
and. . .

A worrying time for
Steve Davis, before
winning the round

Beating Cliff Thorburn in the 1981 World Championship semi-final

Steve Davis and Doug Mountjoy before the final

left Moments after winning the world title

right Steve Davis enjoys a well-earned rest

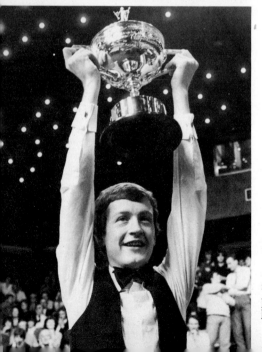

left Steve Davis, World Champion, 1981

right The trick is to pot the black without killing the assistant

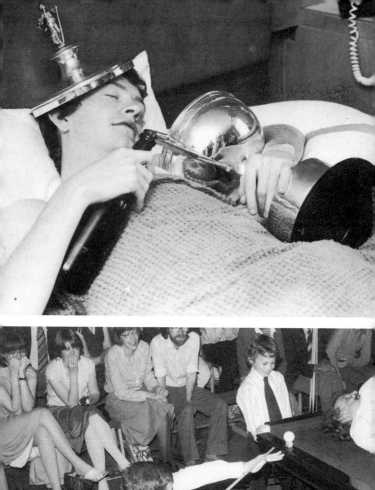

Steve Davis in action

Behind the scenes, bookmakers were swamped with big bets on White. The judges – good, bad and indifferent – were unanimous for a change that he was a certain winner.

Corals stood to lose so much on Jimmy that they telephoned Barry to ask him whether I could win. Barry told them a few white lies and said: 'Yes, he's got a chance.' And in putting the receiver down added '– not really!' All of a sudden, I was the bookmakers' best friend.

It seemed my task was impossible when Jimmy raced into a 3–1 lead at the first interval. But from then on, I won six frames in a row to become the first player in the history of Pontin's tournaments to win both as an amateur and as a professional.

Reardon was brimming with compliments. He opened his newspaper column the following week saying, 'Steve Davis has just achieved the impossible. Remember the name! He is bound to reach the very top.'

Coming from Reardon, that was the highest praise possible. Rex Williams referred to it as 'perfect snooker' and all Dennis Taylor could say was 'Poor Jimmy, he didn't see a ball.'

For me, I considered it one of my finest demolition jobs, although, to be fair to Jimmy, the thirty-point start he received went against him rather than for him. It put him in the wrong frame of mind. It gave him a false sense of security. I think this fact was emphasized in the 1981 world championships when, not expected to win, he fared enormously better against me.

Jimmy has lots of natural ability and is similar to Higgins in character. An exciting player to watch when in full flight and has earned the nickname Whirlwind.

Success at Pontin's was followed immediately by a flood of bookings for exhibitions and my fee went up from fifty pounds a night to a hundred – in some cases, a hundred and fifty a night. All very nice, but I was still waiting for my first win in a major professional tournament.

As some light relief, I joined up with the late Ronnie Dukes and took part in television's pro-celebrity series. Ronnie was the best of the celebrities and won a prize for the highest break. I didn't play too well, although I enjoyed a good laugh.

The series was produced by Yorkshire Television, and their commentator Ted Lowe sat in a makeshift box close to the table. In one match, John Spencer needed only a black to complete the century. As he cued up on the ball, he could hear Ted Lowe in the background confidently whispering, 'And John has a very simple, straightforward black for the hundred . . .'

Being a great joker, John couldn't let the moment pass without stirring Ted up. He rose from his shot, chalked his cue and suddenly took aim on the yellow. Ted almost swallowed the microphone. And John burst out laughing as he heard Ted struggling for the right words to get himself off the hook.

Events of this sort and the nightly exhibition matches all help to take the strain off continual tournament play. Some exhibition matches have turned out ridiculously funny, and I have yet to play at a club that doesn't have its own resident comedian determined to take the mickey out of me no matter what I try.

On one hilarious visit to Margate I took some awful stick for more than an hour from an inebriated customer way up the back in the dark. As he kept nattering on, I couldn't wait for the trick shots to come around to get my revenge, as I have one shot up my sleeve for such occasions.

For this particular shot I always need an assistant from the audience, and being a good sport, my intoxicated friend accepted the invitation and came down to the table to show himself in the light. I explained to him that he was required to lie flat on his back on the table, hold the lump of chalk between his teeth and that I would place the black ball delicately on top of the chalk. Having made himself comfortable, and with the chalk and ball close to his mouth, I went to the top cushion, rested the white ball on top of another cube of chalk and attempted to pot the black without killing my volunteer.

Just as I was about to take aim, the prostrate comedian suddenly shifted on the table and his jacket flicked open to reveal a large bottle of whisky tucked away in an inside pocket. On seeing the bottle, the audience fell about laughing, and I joined them, with tears rolling down my face.

Five times I failed to pot that black, but the crowd loved every minute of it. They kept urging me on, although I'm not sure whether they wanted me to pot the ball or hit the comedian.

Hecklers are always good fun. I love club banter. Some of the gags that come pouring out are fantastic – a goldmine for scriptwriters. Sometimes even the people who prepare the tables have a marvellous sense of humour.

One of my first exhibition matches was at a college in Hampstead in support of Rag Week. The table appeared to have a good cloth, and the lighting was fair. Yet I should have guessed all was not well when the man running the show took me to one side and whispered that I might find the cushions a little slower than I had been used to.

Slower? This was the snooker understatement of the century. They were non-existent. Just thick strips of dead rubber. When a ball hit them with any reasonable force, it either went thud and stopped, or went thud and shot up and practically hit the lights.

One night at Peterborough, while playing Mark Wildman, the audience seemed so intoxicated we decided to test their powers of observation. Instead of using the usual white ball, we produced one that had been specially weighted so that when it struck it would never follow a straight line. It would curve off to the right or left, like the bias on the woods they use to play bowls.

The result was incredible. The crowd were so plastered we played a whole frame with the white ball and no one even noticed.

On one visit to Sheffield, it was the referee and not anyone from the crowd who got into the act. He was wearing a new pair of white gloves and just as he was respotting the black for the first time, the ball slipped from his fingers and smashed into the reds.

They were so well spread out that I could have taken a unique opportunity to knock in a hundred – thanks entirely to the referee splitting the pack for me!

On one visit to Windsor panic broke out when I was well into a match against a local amateur. Someone noticed that a panel in the ceiling was bulging badly. In a short time water started to drip on the floor. The swelling got so large that a member of the club picked up the half-butt and started to prod the offending area. Within seconds, the bulge burst and an avalanche of soggy tiles came pouring down, threatening to bury the startled fellow on the floor.

Over the years, I've played in hundreds of clubs, but I can truly say this is the only one in which I have literally brought the house down!

Another night John Spencer and Ray Reardon almost suffered heart failure when they arrived for an exhibition match in the north. The club secretary proudly met them at the door and said, 'We've spared no expense to bring you here, gentlemen. We've even sent the cloth to the cleaners.'

Reaching the table, the players were confronted by a pale sheet of white where the green baize should have been, the dye having been completely washed out in the local laundrette.

During the summer of 1979, I filled in a few times for Spencer and Reardon, giving exhibitions around the Pontin's holiday camps. I also found time to beat Cliff Wilson in the final of the North Ormsby tournament in Middlesbrough, but not without a gigantic struggle and a dramatic sudden-death play-off on a respotted black.

Up to four hundred Teessiders were packed in the room and all you could hear was the crash of pint glasses as they hit the floor. My father and Barry and a handful of supporters drove up to encourage me.

By the time the game reached 3–3 and entered the final frame, the crowd was evenly split between us. I thought I had lost the match when Cliff was left a simple pink – but he missed it.

Hardly believing my luck, I got down and potted a length-of-the-table pink, and then followed up with the black to level the scores, which meant the black had to be respotted.

At this point, Cliff turned to me and said, 'Steve, we've got this far, why don't we split the money – £750 each?'

I knew everyone's attention was focused on us, so I smiled and shook my head. Cliff was surprised. I could see it written in his face. He won the toss and promptly got down and recklessly tried to cut the black in off its spot. A suicidal shot.

Obviously, he felt that if he could pot the black from its spot, he would put me in my place. Not surprisingly, the black missed the pocket, trundled across the table and ended a foot away from the opposite bag, leaving me with the simplest of shots to win the match 4–3.

So I pocketed a cheque for a thousand pounds, and Cliff went home with five hundred. My decision not to split with him had been more than justified, as was my decision to stay in town that night rather than travel back with my supporters in Barry's Mercedes.

The story goes that halfway home some terrible smells started emanating from the rear. It became apparent that all was not well in the back seat. Barry couldn't lower the window because his speed was so fast the draught would have been unbearable. He had no alternative but to pull into the Watford Gap service station and get out for a breath of fresh air.

All five marched off to the cafeteria and one of them, Ronnie Radley, went to the counter and ordered double beans on toast. Barry heard him and couldn't believe it.

He turned to Ron and said, 'Are you trying to be funny?'

'It's not me, Barry,' replied Ron, 'but it's getting so bad in the car that I must be in a position to strike back!'

8 Romford's Naked Ape

To beat Cliff Thorburn was my next aim. He, more than anyone else, was the player I wanted to nail. In fact, I really believed my chance had arrived when I flew out to Toronto for the Canadian Open championships on Thorburn's native territory.

After beating Jimmy White 9–3 for an encouraging start, I progressed to the quarter-finals and came up against 'target man' Thorburn, now well supported by his patriotic countrymen.

I was so relaxed when the match opened that I went straight into a century break. The beginning I had dreamed of, though by the end of the session we were level at 4–4. This turned out to be crucial, because I would have been 5–3 in front, or even 6–2, if I had played better positional shots on the colours.

Thorburn is a tough, dour opponent. His concentration is phenomenal. He loves a good fight, so I knew I could expect a fierce scrap from then on, particularly in front of his fans. I was right. He took no risks, was extremely precise in all he did, gradually took command and beat me 9–6. I was left to eat my way out of my depression with one of those massive steaks that are a speciality in Canada.

More than ever, I now knew that Thorburn was far from invincible. I told myself I ought to beat him on class alone. But class wasn't enough. I needed to be a harder match-player. Terry Griffiths met him in the final of the Canadian championship and fared little better than I did.

Once back on British soil, I prepared for the Coral United

Kingdom championship, a tough, competitive event held at the Guildhall in Preston, and second only to the world championships in prestige.

I opened up against John Dunning, a useful player from Leeds who had gained many notable scalps earlier in his career. Apart from a ninety-one break to take the first frame, John was rarely in the picture and I beat him 9–3. It was later revealed that John had played right through the second session with severe pains in his chest, believed to be a minor heart attack.

With Dunning eliminated, I then faced the formidable challenge of defending champion Doug Mountjoy. It proved a tremendous match. Doug went in front 4–3 at the end of the afternoon session, with me playing far below my best.

During the interval I took a few pounds off Barry while playing crib, and returned to the table fresh and determined to produce the quality snooker of which I knew I was capable.

This proved good relaxation. All of a sudden, everything clicked. Though Doug won the opener, I dominated the rest of the match, winning six frames in a row to triumph 9–5.

On leaving the table, John Williams, the senior tournament referee, paid me a kind compliment that I shall never forget. The popular Welshman said that this was the finest exhibition of snooker he had seen since Joe Davis at his peak.

To make me feel even happier, Bruce Donkin, managing-director of Riley's, the cue and table manufacturers, and a close friend of Joe Davis, was standing alongside, and agreed with all that John had said.

At this point, Barry decided to get me more publicity by backing me down to 3–1 favourite to win the title. Next day, the media latched on to this betting news and made the point that I was being more heavily backed than even Higgins, Griffiths and Spencer.

Suddenly, I suppose, the public were sitting up and asking, 'Who is this bloke Steve Davis they all want to back?' Mission accomplished!

Unfortunately, the tactics didn't work out so well on the table. In my next match, I faced the bearded John Virgo in the quarter-finals. Again I made a sound start with a fifty-four for the first frame, but John was in excellent form and squeezed me out by nine games to six.

Bristling with confidence, he told reporters, 'I am now sure I can win the title.' And he did.

In all my thousands of snooker matches, my most embarrassing moment came during that game against John. While he was calmly putting together a match-winning break, I went to rest my cue despondently on a row of chairs, but to my horror it dropped from my hands and clattered on the floor.

This must have disturbed John's concentration, but, being a good professional, he handled it well and went on to win the frame. It's the only time in my life when I've really wanted an opponent to make sure he potted a ball against me.

By this time, however, I was able to console myself to some extent with the knowledge that whoever beat me usually went on to win the tournament or finish a respectable runner-up.

Perhaps I just needed more improvement in my play, and a little more of the killer instinct. It is all right being the nice guy at a party or in a crowd, but once on the table, it is important to find a ruthless streak. Without it, subtle skills and natural talent are definitely not enough. A player must never take it easy at the table. It would be ridiculous for me to be thrashing, say, Terry Griffiths, and then think, 'He's a nice bloke' – and go easy on him. I have that killer instinct now. The public have noticed, too. Hardly a tournament goes by without letters coming in addressed to 'Steve Davis, the surgeon'.

Yet that doesn't mean that when the game is over, my opponent and I can't chat and enjoy a drink at the bar, although I prefer to keep myself to myself and my close friends.

Though the snooker lads are great fun, I don't think it is a good idea to be too friendly with any particular player because this might – just might – affect my attitude to him during a match.

My disappointment at being knocked out of the Corals United Kingdom championships was short-lived. I stayed at the Crest Hotel in Preston and ended up by making a date with their receptionist Helen Rogan, who later became my regular girlfriend.

Hardly surprising, I lost all interest in the final between John Virgo and Terry Griffiths, and missed all the controversy when John turned up late and was docked two frames. I was having much more fun at a disco.

To balance the disappointment of losing, I decided it was time to buy a new car, for the Maxi was now cracking up with 75,000 miles on the clock. I plumped for a brand new red Rover 3500, demolishing my building society account in one clean sweep.

It was necessary not only to have a big car to cope with the mileage, but to have a classier one to go with the 'image'.

Yet even at this stage, there was no deliberate effort to alter my lifestyle. It all began to happen quite naturally. Besides the new car, I also improved the standard of my wardrobe, both in quantity and quality. A high standard of dress was now a necessity.

Just a week after Preston I was flying out to India with six other professionals to bake under the midday sun in the Bombay Open.

Conditions were not perfect for snooker, but John Virgo maintained his marvellous form to beat Thorburn in the final – after Thorburn had again disposed of me in the semis.

Most of the fortnight was spent cooling off around the hotel pool – and darting to the toilet. All the players agreed that the hospitality from the Indian people was excellent.

By now, 1979 was fading fast and Barry, in one of his crystal-gazing moods, said he was convinced 1980 was to be my year. He reckoned I now had all that was necessary to win a major tournament. Mind you, I seem to remember he predicted this every year.

Just to strengthen this forecast, I made my third maximum at precisely 10.45 p.m. on New Year's Day, my second having been completed while practising at the Commonwealth Club, Blackpool in September. We had no doubt that this latest maximum was the first of the decade!

This put me in the perfect frame of mind for my third consecutive Lucania Pro-Am title a fortnight later when I faced Dennis Taylor in the final after removing Higgins in the semis.

As the final was held at Romford on Dennis's birthday, Barry arranged for a huge cake to be carried in with up to fifty candles burning on top. Dennis saw the joke, but didn't enjoy his snooker so much. The match was played over fifteen frames, seven in the afternoon and eight in the evening. If Dennis expected any presents, he got none – apart from a few snookers.

With the afternoon session over, I was six-nil up and felt I couldn't miss a ball. The pockets looked as big as buckets. Barry had invited a hundred guests to a party downstairs and was a bit worried the game would end early and ruin the evening. In a bit of a sweat, he came up to me and said, 'Look, I've never asked you to do this before, but please do me a favour . . . Let Dennis have one. If you don't, it's going to wreck everything.'

He had no chance. I was itching for revenge for the world championship defeat and I told him: 'There is nothing I wouldn't do for you, but never ask me to lose a frame of snooker.'

Then, just to underline my feelings, I returned in the evening and won the next two frames, trying even harder than ever. This win earned me the Lucania Pro-Am title for the third year in a row – a hat-trick which gave me a lot of satisfaction. Because it finished early, Dennis and I played five exhibition frames. Barry joined in the fun by offering a pound a point to the player with the highest break to be passed on to Cancer Research. The very next frame, I knocked in one of 110.

Like any other form of sport, snooker can be a cruel game. You can be flying high one day, and down on the ground the next. Straight from the Romford jamboree, I went next morning to the British Gold Cup tournament in Bristol. I was involved in a three-man qualifying group, along with Tony Meo and Roy Andrewatha. Each of us played the other over three frames, with only the winner of our group going through to the competition proper.

Meo beat me 2–1 in three sparkling frames of snooker and, although I beat Andrewatha in the next game, Meo topped the group and I was back in my car and heading for London. Besides the obvious disappointment at being ejected, my pride was hurt because I felt three frames in a round-robin tournament were hardly enough for the better player to prove his superiority.

Within a month I had put the record straight. Tony and I met in the final of the invitation pro-am tournament at the Louth Town and Country Club in Lincolnshire, an event I later renamed the First Aid Cup. Tony had a stomach upset and was physically sick during the interval, while I felt like death warmed up with tonsillitis. Somehow I managed to win 8–3, but all I wanted to do was swallow some pills and get home to bed.

After all these matches against the top British players, Barry decided to stage a different type of event at Romford which would allow me to take a close look at the overseas stars I could be drawn against in the world championships.

So on 1, 2 and 3 February Steve Davis played the Rest of the World at Romford. Australian Eddie Charlton came first. He turned professional in 1963 and has dominated the Australian scene ever since, both on the table and through his business links with sponsors and television companies. Since 1964, he has won the Australian professional championships every year, except in 1968, but has yet to win the world title or a major tournament in Britain.

I still don't know him well, but when we first met at Pontin's, with me still an amateur, he brushed past and said, 'Hello, champ.'

Charlton's great strength is in his concentration. He doesn't possess the ability of Thorburn, and I don't think he's got the range of shots necessary to win the world championship. Yet for all these shortcomings, he remains a tough and resilient competitor. At Romford, he sailed off with a ninety break against me to win the first frame. But from then on, I didn't let him see a ball and I beat him five frames to one.

Barry lined up Thorburn for me on the second day in a match over fifteen frames. As usual, Thorburn played hard, methodical snooker, but it all proved academic in the end as I beat him eight games to six.

Even though I had beaten him at Romford, where I obviously played my best snooker, the psychological boost was tremendous. I had climbed a mountain. I had lost to Thorburn three times previously and now I had finally beaten him.

Barry was delighted. He had backed me to complete the hat-trick, and only South African Perrie Mans stood in our way. For the first four frames, there was not a problem in sight. Perrie was an absolute pushover. He couldn't pot a ball.

Then, all of a sudden, I found myself struggling. For the first time in my life I experienced the well-known Perrie Mans spoiling tactics at first hand. It was something I should have noticed much earlier and found a way of combating.

Perrie is an excellent potter and one of the hardest hitters of a ball in the game. Few will forget his memorable pink against Reardon in the 1978 world final when he screwed back the length of the table for position on the black. He shows no compunction in smashing the balls all over the table, as he is no great positional player. His biggest asset is his unorthodoxy, and he is a far better safety player than people give him credit for. Those who play him can never predict with any confidence what he intends to do next. Although Perrie has neither the precision nor the consistency to establish himself as a constantly good player, he will always pull off the odd surprise.

I must confess he confused me a bit at Romford, and I had to battle fiercely to win the match by five games to three. I put it all down to improving my education.

With this international hat-trick safely in the bag, I decided to settle for a spot of relaxation again, entering the United Kingdom Billiard championships in Leeds, eventually beating Sid Hood for the right to meet world champion Rex Williams and take the inevitable thrashing.

Barry and a handful of Romford supporters knew there was no way in which I could beat Rex, but still fancied a day in Leeds where we were itching to try out a new 'infallible' numbers system on the roulette-wheel.

Despite the massacre, I was even more embarrassed when Rex complained about the noise coming from behind a curtain just outside the main match area. Though billiards is a great game, it can, at times, become boring to follow for those other than purists, and especially so when one player is being murdered, as I was.

Barry and one of my supporters couldn't bear to watch and had slipped outside to play on a Space Invader machine. From the noise on the other side of the curtain, it was clear they were enjoying a far closer game than Rex and I were.

With Rex into another 'million' break, he turned to me and said, 'That's your manager out there making all the noise, isn't it?' Feeling a little guilty, I could only agree and apologize and wish I was with them having some fun.

The day's highlight without doubt involved one of my frisky supporters who sneaked away with a seventeen-year-old girl from behind the snack-bar.

Barry joked that even the RSPCA would refuse to let her

in as a dog. She reminded him of the only two good things that came out of Leeds – great footballers and beautiful women. The girl in question refused to let on what position she played.

Anyway, they disappeared together, returning around ten o'clock, just in time to join us as we were warming up to take on the casino.

'Sorry, mate,' said Barry. 'No women allowed. This is serious business. She'll have to go.'

Afraid to lose her, my supporter handed her his hotel room keys and promised to be back with her in an hour or so.

In the meantime, I was agreeing with Barry that I had picked up money for old rope in being slaughtered by Rex and with great optimism set off to break the bank.

Sadly, the system proved a catastrophic flop, and four hours later we made our way back to the hotel. We were all on the same floor, and the room used by our love-struck Don Juan came first.

'Bet she's not in there,' said Barry.

The door was unlocked, so we pushed it open and there she was, all tucked up and fast asleep.

At this point, with all of us peering in, the supporter turned to Barry and said to him, 'Look, mate, you've been good to me in the past, she's all yours.'

Barry and I fell back against the wall in hysterical laughter, and Barry told him that he had suffered enough bad luck for one evening.

The supporter, a tired fifty-one, clearly couldn't cope with this energetic young girl and was desperate for someone to replace him. Anyway, Barry and I left him in the corridor to sort out his problems and settled down for the night.

It was at breakfast next morning when the full story came to light. Barry and I were told that at six o'clock, the naked supporter emerged from his room completely exhausted, tiptoed down the hall to another supporter, and pleaded with him to swop places.

The supporter agreed to take over, but only if the girl went to his room. The girl agreed, so the first supporter said he would stand outside in the hall, behind a pillar, to make sure the coast was clear.

Unfortunately while standing well out of sight, his heel swung back and struck a bedroom door. Within seconds, a bleary-eyed man opened up and found our supporter standing in front of him, totally naked except for his shoes.

Quick as a flash, the Romford man said, 'Good morning, sir, just checking: was it the *Daily Express* or the *Star*?'

With so many competitions, exhibition matches and endless hours of travelling to suffer, such funny moments are priceless gems to cherish and recall.

However, there was nothing to smile about a week later when I gave Jimmy White ten start in the Demmy Pro-Am at the Potters Club in Salford, and lost 5–3.

Barry had already placed large bets on me to win when I turned up to tell him I felt rough with flu. As if this was not bad enough, the Playboy Club received a generous donation after the match, and we *all* went home as sick as pigs. Still, you can't win them all.

9 Barry Keeps His Word

Of course, all through February and March, the only real topic of conversation was the world championships. When the draw was made on television I was delighted to hear that if I managed to get through the qualifying rounds I would again meet Patsy Fagan in the first round proper, with the winner going on to face the defending champion Terry Griffiths.

Chris Ross was my preliminary opponent as I set out on the long and arduous trail. Of Scottish descent, Chris was living in Surrey and three years earlier had won the All-England championships. We played at the Romilly Forum in Stockport and, as Chris had suffered from a nervous complaint for a couple of years, it was no surprise when I beat him comfortably by nine games to two.

Next came Paddy Morgan, a competent Irishman who had settled in Australia in the mid-1970s and, in my opinion, was the only player out there who could live with Eddie Charlton. Aware of Morgan's reputation, I was determined not to let him settle. My form was particularly good at that stage and, with several breaks of sixty and seventy, I destroyed him nine frames to nil, which enabled me to enter the competition proper for the second time.

On returning to The Crucible, I was now far better prepared. I knew what to expect. I knew all about the atmosphere, the crowds and the television cameras. I also knew I had a tough, demanding draw.

Patsy Fagan came first. His problems with the rest were apparently behind him and he was reputed to be playing a lot better again. To keep me on my toes, Patsy collected the first two frames, with me missing several simple shots mainly through an attack of nerves.

If I was having trouble on the table, up on the balcony my father was suffering even more. Unlike me, however, he had the opportunity to leave and go for a walk, which he did, hoping that with him not being there I would recover. Dad was adopting the ostrich technique, burying his head in a pint of sand at the bar.

By the third frame, I had knuckled down, was used to the speed of the table, and felt at ease in the atmosphere. I eventually beat Patsy by ten games to six.

At last, I could truly say I was in the big time. One of the final sixteen competitors in the most important snooker event in the world, and with a chance to make a name for myself, having drawn Terry Griffiths in the next round. All eyes were guaranteed to be on our match, especially with so much television coverage.

Terry had won the title on merit the previous year with some tremendous snooker. He enjoyed the experience, and the many financial fruits of his success. Later on, he won the Benson and Hedges Masters, the Benson and Hedges in Ireland, was runner-up in the Canadian Open and runner-up in the Corals United Kingdom championship. No matter what tournament Terry played in during his year as champion, he either won, or got extremely close. Yet, in an interview on the day before our match it became apparent for the first time that he was starting to feel the pressure of having to defend the crown.

A few weeks earlier, Barry had suggested that it might be to our advantage to invite Terry down to Romford for a challenge match over twenty-five frames. Terry had played at Romford a few times before. He knew the table, knew the surroundings, and was always made to feel welcome by the locals, who genuinely appreciated his delicate artistry.

There was no reason for him to feel a stranger in a foreign

camp. Yet, despite having all these points on his side, he played well below what was expected of him. At one stage, I led him ten frames to nil, virtually without missing a ball, and at the end trounced him 13–2.

In a Press interview later, Terry admitted, 'I've been playing well lately, but on that form no one in the world could live with Steve Davis. He played exceptionally well.'

When we walked into The Crucible for our crucial match, I felt like whispering in his ear, 'Don't forget last time, Terry.'

Whether thoughts of that Romford result did flow back, I shall never know. All the record books will show is that I raced into a seven-nil lead. To be frank, I was amazed to see how much his arm shook in those first two frames. Though it is usual for the cueing arm to quiver on the opening shots, it is something which generally disappears once a player starts concentrating. In Terry's case, it didn't.

Despite his attack of nerves, Terry still won the last frame of the first session to go to bed trailing by seven frames to one. Though enjoying this enormous lead, I still felt I had not played anywhere near my best. I merely potted everything that he left on, and gained in confidence shot by shot. I felt very pleased with myself.

Next morning, the newspapers were plastered with head-lines predicting the end for Griffiths. 'Champ on way out'... 'Terry on the rack'... 'Champ on brink of defeat'.

Well, Terry can't have read any of them. Or, if he did, then they only served to recharge and inspire him. He began the second session with much more zest and enterprise, although I succeeded in extending my lead to 10–3 before he produced his finest snooker. Slipping into his rhythm, Terry won the last three frames of the day to end the session 10–6 in arrears.

The pendulum was starting to swing. Suddenly I was feeling the pressure of being expected to win, now that I had established such a commanding lead. A glance at the score-board told me I still needed three of the remaining nine frames for victory, and the result was far from a foregone conclusion.

Going down for breakfast at the hotel next morning, I noticed that the papers had now slightly changed their views. Terry was no longer a dead duck. The headlines were suddenly raving about the 'Great Griffiths fightback!' I couldn't argue against this opinion, for the facts were there for all to see. But I was still confident I would win, though Terry was obviously performing a lot better and now had the psychological advantage of going out to play with nothing to lose.

With breakfast over, I went to find Barry, as there was something important I had to discuss with him. In the years since I first met Barry, he has become more than just a manager and a friend. He is like an older brother to me.

I said to him, 'Barry, tell me that I won't be a mug if I lose this one.'

'Don't be stupid,' he said.

'That's not good enough,' I replied. 'You have to say the actual words.'

Barry looked at me, puzzled, but I was deadly serious. I realized I had reached the most important moment in my playing life, and I needed just the slightest reassurance from a friend.

Looking me straight in the eye, Barry said, 'Steve, you won't look a mug if you blow it.'

That was good enough for me. I said 'Fine', and we went off to The Crucible. As I walked through the streets, people in shops and bus queues shouted words of good wishes and the whole of Sheffield seemed to know who I was. Deep inside, I knew I could win. I kept reminding myself that I had a four frame buffer. I also knew that if I lost, the cynics would soon be jumping around, sniping away that 'Davis couldn't keep it up' or his 'bottle went'. That's why it is always so important to have good friends and good supporters. There were enough in the theatre when Terry and I resumed at eleven o'clock.

Well, Terry enjoyed a dream start. In the first frame, he fluked a red and made a break of ninety-five. In the second, he knocked up a break of seventy, closing the gap to two frames, at 10–8.

Looking up towards the balcony, I noticed that my father and Barry couldn't stand the tension and had left for the bar. I later learned that Barry was in such a state of panic that he tried to light a cigarette when he already had one in his mouth. Then he put down the second one, grabbed his pint of lager and tried to drink it, with the cigarette still smouldering between his lips.

I was fully satisfied with my form, but Terry seemed to be getting the better opportunities, and we reached the mid-session interval locked tightly at ten games apiece.

Before the match, Barry and I had agreed that he would not visit me in the dressing-room while the game was in progress. He's a bit superstitious that way. He reckoned my defeat to Dennis Taylor the previous year had something to do with his calling on me during the match. Anyway, with the score at 10–10, my father kept putting more and more pressure on Barry to visit me. He told Barry he had stacks of information on where I was going wrong and that he wanted him to pass the lot on to me. I am convinced there are times when there is more mental strain on my father and Barry just watching, than there is on me out on the table playing.

I had been sitting in my dressing-room just three minutes or so when who should turn up, but Barry, and with the most original excuse for coming in. Though I had lost seven frames in a row, I was still feeling good. If anything, I was more relaxed now that I no longer carried on my shoulders the pressure of being expected to win. As Barry breezed in, I happened to be singing and whistling. This surprised him, and he said, 'I've just come down to find out how you're feeling.'

'I'm okay,' I said.

'Are you sure?'

'Yes.'

'Right,' he said, 'then I'll go.'

So he left, and went back to my father.

'How is he?' dad asked.

'He's whistling!' Barry replied.

'Did you tell him what I told you?'

'Yes,' said Barry.

My dad immediately relaxed, and stopped chewing on his cigar . . .

Later that night, while watching the day's highlights on television, I was amused to hear a well-known commentator explaining to viewers how Steve Davis's game had improved after a 'dressing-room ticking off' from his manager.

The vital twenty-first frame was a cliffhanger. One minute it was Terry's, the next it was mine. I believe the whole match hinged on Terry's decision to pot the last red into the top left-hand pocket. The blue was partly covering the hole, and it was debatable whether the red would squeeze past it. If the red had dropped, Terry was a certainty for the frame. He struck the red well, and it hit the cushion just before the blue, cannoned into the blue, but refused to go in. To be honest, in Terry's situation, I would have played exactly the same shot.

With the red at my mercy over the pocket, I made one of the most important clearances of my life. It produced a great feeling inside me to know that I could hit back after losing seven frames in a row. Stung into action, I quickly got among the reds in the next frame and cleared up with a break of 116 to go 12–10 in front.

The twenty-third frame was another see-saw thriller. Always in front, I potted the yellow to go twenty-six points ahead, only to fail on the green, which meant Terry needed a snooker. He found one quickly, potting the green and then cleverly leaving me behind the pink, totally obscuring me from the brown. I played off one cushion, hit the brown, but almost died as I saw the white go in-off.

Worse still, the brown ended up near the centre pocket. With the blue close to the 'D', Terry needed only to pot the brown and send the white off the top cushion to leave it three-quarters of the way up the table. This would have virtually guaranteed him the frame.

To my amazement, Terry played a terrible shot. He thumped the white so hard it ended up touching the baulk cushion, about the worst place on the table from which to pot the blue. A few safety shots followed before Terry played a particularly bad one, leaving the blue literally hanging over the 'green' pocket. I potted this one, and added the pink to win the match by thirteen frames to ten after a tense and gruelling battle.

The pressure that accumulates in a match of such intensity can never be adequately described in words. There is no way to express the thrill that goes on inside. I jumped so high I was in danger of hitting the roof. I had beaten the world champion. Even in this cauldron of excitement, I was cool enough to realize that I had broken a great professional barrier. From now on, I was established as a true, top-class player.

Before the final session, while walking from our hotel to The Crucible, Barry had promised that if I could beat Terry he would jump fully clothed into the ornamental pond in the heart of the city. Jubilant on the way back, I made sure he kept his word.

Terry left Sheffield saying he was going straight home to Llanelli to put in more practice. But when I went down to breakfast next morning, I found that he had left me a note wishing me 'the best of luck' for the rest of the tournament. A nice, friendly gesture which I very much appreciated.

I spent the day collecting four shirts from the laundry and putting in some practice for my clash with Higgins in the quarter-finals. All of a sudden, too, I was experiencing the full blast of Press and television pressure. The telephone didn't stop ringing and I was swamped by reporters. In one instance I was badly misquoted by a national newspaper whose reporter claimed I had said that 'People love to hate me because I'm playing perfectly, and I know it.' This upset me at the time and it put me on my guard when talking to Press people in the future.

The first session with Higgins produced snooker of the highest calibre. One newspaper claimed the match was so breathtaking the crowd were applauding with relief when it was all over. During this magic spell, I achieved a total clearance of 136 to equal the highest of the championships made on the first day by Kirk Stevens, for which each of us received a cheque for five hundred pounds.

In one of his dazzling moments in that opening session, Alex produced a spectacular break of 122, and gained the first genuine chance of a championship maximum, with ten thousand pounds of the sponsor's money staring him in the face. Unfortunately for Alex, the green was near the bottom cushion. It was almost impossible to acquire a good angle on it after getting slightly out of position on the yellow while potting the black. Alex was forced to try a long double into the top pocket, but missed. Nevertheless, it was a superb break, and there was no one watching, in the theatre or glued to a television set, who wanted him to succeed more than I did.

Higgins blamed his new tip. He said it did not bite properly when he applied a lot of 'side' on the white ball to pot the yellow and seek a good position on the green. I don't know about that, but it certainly didn't affect the rest of his performance. I was always struggling to keep with him after the first session.

We went to lunch at 4–4, and by the end of the second session I had dropped two behind at 9–7. My fate was finally sealed in the last session when Alex, enjoying a feast of luck, pulled away to win 13–9. Luck is all part of the game, and I am not taking the slightest credit away from Alex's magnificent effort. All through the game Alex showed surprising restraint and self-control. He played his best snooker for years.

Naturally disappointed, I accepted that learning how to lose was all part of my apprenticeship. I was pleased with my overall performance and was sure that I left Sheffield that year a much better player. Barry agreed. He felt we had both learnt a lot about coping with the pressures of a world championship campaign. The fun we had had, even in defeat, was to prove the springboard to further enjoyment.

Higgins had promised his supporters that this was to be the Year of the Hurricane. It definitely looked that way. Twice in the early stages of his final against Cliff Thorburn he held a four-frame lead. Then he slipped. I believe Alex saw the winning-post too early and reverted to his more familiar attacking game. This change of tactics played straight into Thorburn's hands, although the Canadian still needed more than one bite of the cherry to take the title out of Britain by eighteen frames to sixteen.

From The Crucible I went to Pontin's, and for the first time in three years came away with nothing to show for my labours. The only consolation was that a lot more people wanted my autograph!

Shortly afterwards, to uphold my tradition of winning at holiday camps, I played in the Warner's Open on Hayling Island and captured the title and a cheque for two thousand pounds. This was the biggest pay-day of my career so far. I beat Brian Watson, of Portsmouth, by five games to one, giving him twenty-one points. Yet the real pleasure in that week was crushing John Virgo 4–0 in the semi-final to stop all the talk of his being my jinx.

I then flew over to Northern Ireland for a few days to play in exhibition matches. Whenever I am out there, I always stay with Bob Kearney, a promoter of snooker matches and an amusing character. For this visit, Bob hired a furniture van in which to carry the table to play my matches. He drove the van, while I crouched in the passenger seat.

Shooting had broken out on the road we intended to use, but Bob said he knew of an alternative route. We drove along it nicely until we both noticed a low bridge looming up in the distance. As we got closer, I became more and more worried that we couldn't get under it. Bob wasn't bothered. He had forgotten he was driving a hired van. He still thought he was in his car.

With the bridge right on top of us, I said to him, in a wretched state of panic, 'Bob . . .' Just that. There was no time for more. He slammed on the brakes, I held tight, but it was too late. We were stuck under the bridge. Bob was livid with himself, and let fly with some colourful Gaelic expletives. At least, they were words I had never heard before.

In front of us, at the other end of the bridge, were two Army vehicles with a dozen soldiers. They were fully armed, but obviously not seriously prepared for battle as they stood laughing their heads off and applauding loudly. Bob then put the van in first gear and we slowly but surely scraped our way clear.

In coming back from Ireland, I looked forward to my first match in the elegant surroundings of the World Sporting Club in London. Sponsored by Gillette, it was a posh, dinner-jacketed affair, with comedian Eric Morecambe a riotous guest of honour. Halfway through the evening Eric was presented with a gold-plated razor, and in response, he said: 'I should like to thank Gillette for this generous gift. I shall treasure it for ever . . .' And he promptly threw it over his shoulder and it landed on the floor some twenty-five feet away.

A four-course meal was followed by a feast of snooker from Alex and me. Again I was sampling an entirely new atmosphere. I was in top form, beginning and ending with century breaks to win the match by four frames to two. Like Eric, both Alex and I were presented with gold-plated razors. I also received a magnificent decanter to make it a memorable night.

At this time, I was still improving. I was invited to play in tournaments like the Wilson Classic and the Benson and

Hedges Masters. I now saw 1980 as a year in which to climb even higher up the ladder of success.

One disappointing setback came in the Lucania Pro-Am championship. Unbeaten for two years at Romford, I suffered the embarrassment of being comprehensively buried in front of my own supporters by Tony Meo. It was my first defeat for sixteen matches. Though I achieved a break of 142, Tony completely outplayed me, winning by five games to one. By coincidence, in the previous week Ray Edmonds had knocked up a break of 153 on the same table against Cliff Wilson, and he also had lost.

In some ways I looked on that hiding by Meo as a form of relief. It took the pressure off me. Being unbeaten at home meant that I was always forcing myself to be at my peak because everyone expected so much from me. I imagine Borg must have felt the same after losing to McEnroe.

Ray Reardon then found he couldn't fulfil his engagements at the Pontin's holiday camps around the Devon area. As I've always enjoyed the holiday camp atmosphere, I leapt at the chance to help him out. I made lots of friends, and started taking an interest in the harmonica. It's a fascinating instrument which now never leaves my side. I find it works far better than any headache tablet in a traffic jam, though for the time being Larry Adler has nothing to fear.

Terry Griffiths had nothing to fear, either, when he gained ample revenge for his world championship defeat by slaughtering me 9–2 in Toronto for my third consecutive Canadian disaster.

At this time my exhibition fees had gone up to two hundred pounds and my diary was full. Some weeks I was so busy that I worked every night, and the odd lunch-time as well. With the miles piling up I began to feel like a human road map. I was definitely an authority on Indian restaurants. Ask any player to name his favourite meal after a night of snooker and he'll tell you it's an Indian curry. Not only for its flavour, but because Indian restaurants are usually the only ones still open around midnight to serve us.

Promoter Ray Davis warmed us up in a different way when he staged the Champion of Champions tournament at the New London Theatre in Drury Lane. Davis had put on countless small snooker tournaments and lunch-time shows, but seemed to find this one a bit too big to handle. The prize-money of twenty thousand pounds was good, but the New London Theatre was hardly the cheapest venue in town. It had plush seating, with a wonderful arena both for the players and for the audience, but the event itself was not televised, and had no sponsor, so the promoter lost a packet.

A lot of complaining went on behind the scenes, and Ray Davis was given fourteen days in which to find the money to pay the players and officials. He promised that every single debt would be settled, and in time all those involved did receive what was due to them.

The Champion of Champions involved two groups of five players in a round-robin contest over nine frames, with the winner of each group meeting in the final. Dennis Taylor was my first opponent and I raced off to a 5–0 winning lead without missing a ball. Because the rules insisted that all players completed the nine frames, Dennis and I had to carry on, but I found it impossible to maintain my momentum and ended up winning by only five games to four.

Kirk Stevens, the colourful Canadian, came next, and although I flagged in the middle, I still won comfortably by five frames to two. Learning from my slump against Dennis, I then kept up my concentration and added the two dead frames to make it a final score of 7–2.

My third opponent was John Virgo, still visibly smarting at being left out of the Benson and Hedges Masters, and looking all set to unleash his fury on me. By the end of the fifth frame, he led 4–1. The standard was never much better than mediocre, and I found it extremely hard to motivate myself.

A clearance of 128 in the sixth frame underlined my inconsistency and emphasized how my mood was changing from minute to minute.

Virgo was definitely not deterred by my temporary fight-back. He drew clear and wrapped it all up by five games to two. Again two dead frames had to be played and I won them both, reducing the final margin to 5–4.

To retain any hope of winning my group, I now had to beat Ray Reardon, and Reardon had to beat Virgo. The Reardon–Virgo duel proved a tense affair. Reardon led 2–0 and 3–1, yet it was Virgo who showed in front when it mattered, by five frames to four.

This meant my match with Reardon was purely academic as far as the group was concerned. Virgo was now assured of finishing on top. Yet, the group's runner-up spot was still to be settled, and as it offered far better prize-money than third place, there was still a good incentive left for me to do well.

Reardon led 3–1 and 4–2 before I took command, and it gave me great pleasure to beat him 5–4. This meant I had earned a cheque for fifteen hundred pounds, plus another for five hundred and the Sam Leitch Memorial Trophy, for achieving the tournament's highest break of 128.

All through the Champion of Champions I knew I was far below my best. Barry realized it, too, and we discussed the reasons thoroughly later. Barry has never tried to tell me how to play, and I would never think of advising him on how to run his business. But he was concerned about my attitude to the game. He felt I wasn't thinking positively enough about it. He told me that I had not only lost to Virgo but, worse still, I had looked like a loser, too.

'With all the talent you have,' he said, 'you still don't believe enough in yourself. I can't understand why. Before you can win a big tournament you must know that you can beat them and, more to the point, you must let them know that you can beat them.'

With this timely piece of advice, Barry made it plain that my attitude was wrong. That no amount of natural talent can succeed at the highest level unless it is supported by the same degree of character. I sat down alone and chewed over what he had said and realized where I was going wrong.

All Barry says to me before a match these days is, 'The best of luck, Steve, and be the guv'nor.' And we both know what that means.

10 Fun at the UK Coral

After having some fun at the World Billiards Championships in Rugby, when I again lost to John Barrie, I moved on to Preston for my next serious contest, the Coral UK Championships, a title I desperately wanted to win.

As Helen lived less than five miles away, I stayed with her and her mum and, as I had spent a fair amount of time in Preston during the previous year since meeting Helen, it was like playing at home. The chance to relax in familiar surroundings away from the bustle of hotel life is a positive plus when it comes to playing in a big tournament. Practice couldn't be neglected either, and I went up to the Commonwealth Club in Blackpool and felt I was playing better than ever. Barry again backed his faith in me, this time to the tune of £650 at 10–1.

Mike Hallett was my first opponent. To be candid, Mike has always shown a great deal of potential, but, so far, has failed to make the transition from being a top amateur to a leading professional. I played very good snooker and beat him 9–1.

Canada's big Bill Werbeniuk loomed up large as my next opponent. Bill turned professional in 1973 and holds the dubious distinction of being the first professional to split his trousers while playing on television. And he wasn't even wearing underpants!

On a more honourable note, Bill has twice reached the quarter-finals in the world championships, and completed a magnificent 142 break in the 1979 tournament. Being perfectly honest, I have never considered Bill one of my more dangerous rivals, though he's never short of grit and determination.

Bill says he suffers from a rare nervous illness which means he has to consume large amounts of lager during his matches to stop him from shaking. All this drinking means that he has to leave the table far more often than any player I know. At Preston we reckoned that although I beat him 9–3 in the match, he beat me 9–2 in visits to the toilet. The taxman has since been the real loser as he has agreed to allow Bill's lager costs as a deductible expense.

I led him 3–1 at the first interval and went into the foyer where a Space Invader machine was clattering away. It was the first time I had seen one at a snooker tournament. I had so much fun on it that I became hooked on video machines and later arranged for three to be brought into my hotel for the 1981 world championships.

I suppose I like them so much because they demand such immense concentration and dexterity, and they free my mind from all the other tensions that might be going on around me.

Barry and I played a game in the foyer at Preston, and while pressing buttons and pulling levers he suddenly accused me of being sloppy and complacent in my play against Werbeniuk. He said that from where he was sitting the score could easily have been the other way around. As he said this, I was blown up on the Space Invaders and he jokingly said to me, 'You're treating those Space Invaders the same way as you're treating Werbeniuk.'

Though annoyed at what he said, deep down inside I had to agree with him. I was taking it too easy on Bill, but sometimes it requires someone else to notice it and drive the point home to you.

When the match resumed, Barry stayed behind in the foyer, still playing the machine. Some ten minutes later, I returned to fetch the orange juice I had left on a shelf there. Without speaking to Barry, I picked up the drink and told a friend to tell him that I had just taken the fifth frame with a break of eighty-three.

From then on, I refused to let myself ease up and marched swiftly into the quarter-finals.

A short time later, Tony Meo was enjoying the same contented feeling, seeing off the defending champion John Virgo by the vast margin of nine frames to one to make it an all-London quarter-final.

The Press were soon writing it up as the battle of the new regime – the showdown of the young hopefuls. With so much publicity and talk surrounding us, the match became very much more than just another snooker contest. Reputations and pride were at stake. It was a crisis point in my career, for I knew that if I lost it would definitely set me back.

The game was played over seventeen frames, with television cameras beaming virtually every shot into the homes of millions. I raced into a 3–1 lead before Tony rallied to level 3–3. We were both feeling the pressure, but I managed to pull in front by six games to three, only for Tony to retaliate again to 6–5, a brilliant burst that included an immaculate 118. On account of his surname, they call Tony the 'cat', and he was certainly digging his claws in.

For me, the twelfth frame was probably the most important of the whole championships. Though of course every frame counts only as one, it was clear that the difference between leading 7–5 and drawing 6–6 could provide a huge phsychological boost. Tony secured a good lead and looked assured of the frame until he got down to play a straightforward blue into the middle pocket. At the same time, however, he was attempting a difficult positional shot to reach the next red. Out of luck, he struck the blue and went in-off.

After a few safety shots, I cleared up brilliantly and it was the last chance Tony had of winning another frame. I believe my clearance did the damage. When, in the deciding frame, I had made two consecutive breaks in the seventies, Tony sportingly held out his hand and conceded the match.

Having lost only nine frames in reaching the semi-finals, I thought I had every right to be pleased with my performance. For the first time in my professional career, I truly believed I could win, though I was slightly nervous that I must be tempting fate through thinking this way. I remembered a time during my amateur days when I was reasonably confident of winning a Pontin's tournament – and I did. I felt it in my bones long before I reached the final.

I must stress that I never approach a match with a defeatist attitude, thinking that I am going to lose. But on the odd occasion I do get that special feeling that I am going to win. And there's a real difference!

In the other quarter-final, Terry Griffiths swept aside Dennis Taylor by nine frames to two, and it was not long before the media were drumming up our game into a needle match, with Terry out to put the record straight for the world championship defeat I had inflicted on him earlier in the year.

I have always felt confident when playing Terry, although there is no specific explanation for this. Perhaps it has something to do with a conversation we had shortly after both of us turned professional. We had just finished a match at Louth when Terry asked me whether I thought he attacked too much. He probably won't even remember saying it, but it has stuck in my mind. I was surprised he asked my opinion, and it is something I would never do myself. I don't believe professionals should go around asking other professionals to comment on the way they play.

Possibly another reason for feeling so confident against Terry is that his style suits me. I know we are supposed to 'play the table and not the man', but I am sure the styles of some players suit certain opponents better than others.

Though the second and fourth frames could easily have gone either way, Terry was never a serious challenger at any other time during the match. I hardly missed a shot. I can't recall an occasion when I ever played better. I stormed into an 8–0 lead in the afternoon, and needed just fifteen minutes to complete the execution by winning the first frame of a drastically curtailed evening session.

My long potting was probably the key to it all. A great confidence-builder. All round my play was devastating – even if I say so myself!

Of all the compliments that appeared in the Press, the one that meant the most to me came from John Pulman. He said, 'For years I have been saying this lad is world class. Now people will have to sit up and take notice.'

Even my dad couldn't find fault with me that day, and this, surely, was the greatest compliment of them all.

Terry told reporters afterwards, 'I have always said that losing nine games to eight is the same as losing nine games to nil. Now I know that is not true. It is the worst possible experience to be whitewashed.'

It was the first time in living memory that anyone could recall a whitewash in the semi-final of a major competition.

Of course, for the final against Alex Higgins, the full rent-a-crowd drove up from Romford. Barry led the brigade, still bubbling about his 10–1 bet. Well aware of their enthusiasm, I asked Barry if he would plead with them to keep their voices down just for once. I thought a lot of noise might rouse supporters in the Higgins camp and consequently help him to raise his game. We all know Alex plays to the crowd more than any other player.

I hurried into a 3–1 lead, but from the noise in the hall you might have thought Alex was winning 4–0. His fans cheered and roared at everything he did.

When the first session ended, I went over to Barry and told him that I couldn't believe Alex was receiving so much vocal support, and that it was time to tell our boys to break loose with the well-known Romford Roar.

Tearing off their gags, the lads accepted these orders with relish. The frustration of having to keep silent was driving them insane. When the match restarted the level of noise was perfectly balanced.

Alex pulled back to 3–2 and then I rammed in a 114 for the sixth frame; a 95 to make it 5–2; and I sailed though the next three frames to go charging 8–2 in front.

But Alex is no quitter. Before I had time to catch my breath he had closed to 8–5. He was set alight and I was glad to win two of the next three frames to finish the first day at 10–6.

My rejuvenated mood continued into the next day when everything I tried came off. Alex, in the meantime, became more and more restless. He sipped, smoked, shuffled, prowled, looked anxious and pensive, and turned his face into a hundred tortured expressions as the tension grew.

Many times he jumped up, hoping I would miss, and then sat down again when I didn't. I'm sure it wasn't designed to put me off because I've always found him to be a scrupulously fair player.

I say this not forgetting that in one isolated incident during our match he did ridiculously claim a foul when referee John Williams inadvertently picked up the white ball from the table instead of the pink from the pocket.

John plainly had a lapse of concentration. It was an error that was totally out of character, beca﹖ John is about the most efficient referee doing this difficult ﹍ ﹍.

The look of horror on John's face was priceless, and I couldn't resist stepping back and laughing at the situation. Alex then argued that it was a foul shot. John quite rightly replied that it was the referee's fault and not mine. But Alex refused to accept this ruling. He continued to protest and my mind quickly went back to the Reardon incident at Ipswich.

Having learnt my lesson on that occasion, I kept well away from the controversy this time, walking out of the arena, and leaving Alex to quote from his Fantasy Island rulebook.

Eventually, I returned to find everything back to normal and I was allowed to continue with my break.

Totally unperturbed I powered on and reached 15–6, needing just one more frame to clinch my first prestige title. At this point, I remembered the chat Barry and I had gone through some time back concerning what I should say at the presentation ceremony when I won my first major event.

Barry had maintained all along that winning a title would give me an excellent chance to mention the people who had supported me in the past, and could also open new doors for fresh contacts in the future.

In order to put the speech over properly in front of the large crowd and the all-seeing television cameras, we had agreed that when I was one frame away from winning, that we should both leave the hall and meet in my dressing-room for a last-minute run-through.

With no realistic chance of being caught, I left the arena and hoped Barry would remember to do the same. A few moments after reaching my dressing room, the door flew open and in rushed Barry.

My first words to him were, 'This could be terribly unlucky, you know. . . .'

And we laughed. To be 15–6 in front and contemplating defeat was the joke of the year.

Returning to the table, I won the frame I needed, despite concentrating more on the speech than on my shots.

The first move I made on receiving the cup was to give it a triumphant kiss, and I held it high above my head and faced those people who had cheered just about every shot I played. It was my small way of saying 'thank you'.

Celebrations were soon being stoked up back at the Crest Hotel. The party continued until the early hours of next day, and my last recollection of the booze-up was seeing one Romford supporter lying flat on his back on the pool table, fast asleep, with the number eight ball stuck in his mouth like a teed-up golf ball!

With a major championship under my belt, and Barry having picked up his winnings, we felt very pleased with ourselves. Corals had to pay both of us. Yet the hospitality and friendliness of the staff definitely contributed to the enjoyment of our first big tournament win.

It was around this time that I bought my parents a house in Plumstead. It was right next door to my dad's sister, and when we heard it was on the market I couldn't let it pass without putting in a bid. Mum and dad couldn't get a mortgage, and I saw it as a great opportunity to thank them in some tangible way for all the sacrifices they made for me while I struggled to reach the top.

Whenever I am not living out of a suitcase, I stay with them at home and share a bedroom with Keith who, though only sixteen when I won the world championships, was big enough to be my bodyguard. He has no ambition to play snooker seriously, but is keeping in touch by working as a table mechanic for Lucania Snooker Clubs.

Winning the Corals United Kingdom championship meant that I had crossed a major bridge. I was a champion instead of being just a promising prospect, but with my new position came new problems. When I first set out as a professional, it was easy. I had nothing to lose. I beat players I was not expected to beat. But then I reached the stage where people expected me to win, and I lost a few games that I should not have lost. With the title in my grasp, I knew I now had to maintain the same high standard whenever and whoever I played. This would mean working extremely hard in every competition. Again I realized that the game is all about believing in yourself and coping with pressure.

Winning the title didn't really sink in until next morning at Helen's home. I spent an hour or two lying awake in bed just thinking about how I got there in the end. It was wonderful to wake up not just as a player, but as a champion.

Financial rewards started drifting in immediately. Even before I left the Guildhall I had signed a cue contract with Riley's worth an estimated £25,000.

I took a complete break from snooker on the Sunday, walking with Helen in the park and, for once, I didn't even bother to look at my cue. It was nice to be able to savour success without having to jump in the car and drive hundreds of miles to an exhibition match.

Monday morning was different. It was back to business in the Wilson Classic tournament, a short drive down the motorway at Bolton. I was up on cloud nine now, and without a care in the world.

Cliff Thorburn was the first head to rest on the chopping-block, and I sliced through him 2–0. David Taylor, the Silver Fox, came next. Another match over three frames, with David nicking the middle one. I was so confident that the pockets looked like saucepans – and I cooked him!

Without raising a sweat, I was already sauntering into the final, a match of seven frames against Dennis Taylor. Dennis failed with a comparatively easy chance to level at 2–2, and from then on, I was never seriously pressed to win 4–1 and push my earnings up to £11,000 in less than a week.

After Bolton, I moved on to Liverpool for a £2,000 challenge match against Alex Higgins over twenty-five frames in a city hotel. Alex managed to creep a little closer than he did in the UK championships, but I confirmed my superiority by beating him 13–10, and so raised my week's earnings to an unbelievable £13,000.

Owing to a full programme of exhibition matches and tournaments, I find all too often that I can't fit in as many charity shows as I would like to. Shortly before Christmas 1980, however, I played Kirk Stevens at Romford and beat him 5–2 for the Joe Davis Memorial Trophy, raising £2,000 for Cancer Research.

Kirk has a wonderful range of shots but, at times, he tends to be more reckless than Alex. With greater care, I am sure he could prove a much stronger opponent.

Not surprisingly, the 1981 Pot Black series passed me by again. This time I didn't even manage to win one frame!

Compensation was just around the corner. Kirk and I clashed again in a challenge match, promoted by estate agent Ivan Cawood at the Albany Hotel in Birmingham. I won 5–3 and earned myself £3,600.

Having tucked both the United Kingdom and Wilson Classic titles under my belt, the Press were now starting to speculate about whether I could pull off the hat-trick by winning the prestigious Benson and Hedges tournament at the Wembley Conference Centre.

The sponsors spare no expense in making this annual contest a superb event. The 1981 tournament involved the world's top twelve players who competed for £20,000 in prize money, of which the winner received £6,000. Benson and Hedges receive their rewards, too, with huge crowds clamouring to attend every session, and plenty of television.

My opening match was against the left-handed South African potting machine, Perrie Mans. On the strength of winning two titles, Corals made me the 7–2 favourite, with Perrie a considerable outsider.

It is quite easy to underestimate Perrie, as I think all the other players would agree. I was guilty of making this very mistake during our match – and I lived to regret it. Perrie's unorthodoxy confused me so much that I lost my rhythm and finally lost the match 5–3. Many players complained that the table ran abnormally fast, but there was no easy way in which I could offer that as an excuse for a terribly disappointing performance.

Almost immediately I packed my bags and set off for Margate, where I was booked for an exhibition match which I had planned to fit in during the tournament. By the end of the night, after many good laughs over my trick shots, and a long exchange of friendly banter with the crowd, the Mans defeat was well flushed from my system.

Regrettably there were no laughs to recall when I faced Alex Higgins a short time later in an exhibition match over twenty-one frames in front of a capacity crowd of eight hundred at a club in Rotherham.

All went smoothly until we arrived at the first interval. Alex then went off for a quick drink and spotted a table-top model of a Space Invader game in the bar. By rights, the interval was to last only twenty minutes, and I returned to the arena when time was up and waited for Alex to come back. But he didn't appear. In fact, a further forty minutes went by, and there was still no sign of him.

Bouts of slow-handclapping broke out, and sections of the crowd shouted their anger. The organizers knew exactly where Alex was sitting but, as far as I could see, no one wanted to take the responsibility for insisting that he returned to the table to resume the game.

In the end, at least one person was so incensed that he reported Alex's conduct to the World Professional Billiards and Snooker Association. When the Association eventually got around to considering the case they dished out their heaviest penalty on record. They ruled that Alex had shown a lack of table manners and fined him two hundred pounds, docked him two points in the seeding list, and warned him that he faced exclusion from the world championships if he stepped out of line again.

I have strong principles about exhibition matches. I always try to turn up on time, dress well, be polite and treat each club with great respect. One has to remember that an exhibition match is probably something a club has looked forward to for many months, and sometimes this is their most important night of the year.

On the subject of dress, people frequently ask me why Alex is allowed to play without a tie when all his opponents are instructed to wear one. The explanation is that Alex has obtained a doctor's certificate which excuses him from the game's strict rules governing what we wear. Alex says he develops a troublesome rash around his neck when he gets hot under the collar from wearing a tie.

I was one of the countless guests when Higgins was hailed the hero on the television programme, *This is Your Life*. Most of us thought Oliver Reed stole the show with his immaculate impersonation of Alex!

11 Pulling out the Stops

On the strength of winning the United Kingdom championship, I started more promotional work for Corals. It meant
touring the country to open betting shops, sign hundreds of
autographs and play snooker exhibitions in the evenings. All
excellent fun in the very best company.

With the tour over, I then flew to Dublin to compete in the
Benson and Hedges Irish Masters. I began impressively by
beating John Virgo 4–3, but then slumped 4–2 to Ray
Reardon in the quarter-finals.

Terry Griffiths went on to win the title, but when the time
arrived for the presentations, the unpredictable Higgins
couldn't be found. When he didn't step up to collect his cheque
as a losing semi-finalist the audience watched in amazement
as John Virgo sprang into action. Quick as a flash he did a
complete circuit of the table in unmistakable Higgins style,
shook hands with the promoter, and went off with the cheque!

No doubt it didn't take Alex long to hear of what happened,
and he soon hastily reappeared to claim what was his.

I had been back in England just a day or two when a girl
representing the Noel Edmunds radio show conned Barry a
treat on the telephone. Their conversation went something like
this . . .

'Is that you, Mr Hearn?'

'Yes.'

'I'm the entertainments secretary of the Brighton Nudist
Club.'

'Yes.'

'We would very much like your star Steve Davis to spend a night with us.'

'Oh, yes!'

'No! No! Nothing like that. We want him for a snooker exhibition.'

'I think that could be arranged.'

'Good. But I must warn you that we are a nudist club and that all our members will be undressed.'

'No problem. Won't affect Steve's game in the slightest. It might even improve his potting!'

'The heating will be turned up, of course, and if possible we'd like Steve to play in a pair of shorts.'

'If the money is right, you can have Steve without the shorts – that's as long as you can find someone to carry his chalk!'

Unable to keep serious any longer, the girl blew her cover. She told Barry the conversation had been recorded, and Barry and I later agreed that it could be used on one of Noel's amusing weekend shows. In fact, we are still waiting to hear it.

We later found out that Barry's secretary Linda Grimstead was also party to the hoax, typical of the laughs we had at the Romford base.

On the run-up to the Yamaha Organs International tournament in the first week of March, I played exhibition matches every night of the week. Every time a different place, just earning, earning, earning.

The Yamaha tournament was staged at the Assembly Rooms in Derby. A short-game tournament which I don't particularly like because I believe the best players can only emerge in matches that last from around seventeen to twenty-five frames, if not more. When the draw was announced, I found myself in the same group as Jimmy White, John Virgo and Cliff Thorburn. On paper it was undoubtedly the toughest group of the four. I responded by assuring myself that the hardest groups usually work out best for me. Perhaps they inspire me, and make me try harder. One thing is certain, a tough draw never deters me.

While in Derby, I accepted an invitation from comedian Tony Dowling, who I had met at the Pontins holiday camps, to stay at his home in Ripley throughout the tournament. Once again, it was like being at home. I played my first game on a Wednesday, which was just as well because the television cameras were in action for the first time. I faced Thorburn in the best of three frames. I took the first, lost the second, and won the third.

This victory over Thorburn gave me particular pleasure and put me in the right frame of mind for my match against Virgo. To be fair to John, when he came out to play I had already completed three frames on the table and was well adjusted to the atmosphere. I beat him 3–0 which, in the circumstances, was not unexpected. He had no time to put his game together.

The only way I could not fail to qualify for the semi-finals was to lose 3–0 to Jimmy White. Jimmy had been attracting a lot of publicity, and the Press were warning me that I would need to be at my best – or prepare for the worst! As it turned out, he played a number of good shots, but his consistency was well below standard. I beat him 3–0 for a clear passage into the semi-finals. What might have seemed a difficult group had become a one-horse race. I couldn't have hoped for a better run through.

By now, a lot of big names had been knocked out. I was to face Dennis Taylor in one semi-final, and Kirk Stevens and David Taylor were to meet in the other.

Again I started as though there was no tomorrow, charging into a commanding 4–0 lead. Dennis recovered a little, pulling back two frames, but then I grabbed the vital seventh one to clinch the match by five games to two. Suddenly, I was safely in the final, and a good pay-day was guaranteed: £10,000 to the winner, £5,000 to the runner-up.

David Taylor had already beaten Kirk, so I knew my

opponent early. David has improved a great deal in the past few years. He actually turned professional way back in 1968, straight after winning the world amateur championships, but the following ten years produced very little for him. His luck then changed dramatically in 1978 when he reached the final of the Coral United Kingdom championships, beating Fagan, Virgo and Higgins before losing to Mountjoy in the final.

His game continued to blossom, and in the 1980 world championships he beat Ray Edmonds, Fred Davis and Ray Reardon before losing to the eventual winner, Cliff Thorburn, in the semi-finals.

Our Yamaha final was played over seventeen frames. After being level at one-all, I seized absolute control and enjoyed a 6–2 lead at the interval. Watching the day's highlights on television later that evening, I had to smile when commentator Clive Everton said, 'And Davis is playing like a celestial vacuum-cleaner.' I was also being called the Romford Robot and the Plumstead Potting Machine!

Coming out for the second session, I quickly won the first two frames and should have clinched the match 9–2. I missed an easy pink and David helped himself to the gift.

This was the first time I had ever seen 'money' written across the face of a ball. I remember getting down, needing only the pink to win, saying to myself, 'Pot this, and it's ten thousand pounds.'

Of course, if you think of a single ball in terms of money, the chances are that you'll miss the shot, which is one good reason why I never played many money matches as a young-ster. I concentrated on winning for the sake of winning, and this is still my motivation.

When a player is as far adrift as David was, he has nothing to lose. Pressure is only on the man trying to cross the winning line.

From 8–2 behind, David patiently clawed his way back to 8–6. I was beginning to miss a few shots, and the crowd were so roused into encouraging him that the referee demanded

silence or he would stop the match. It was nice to note that
the people making the noise at the wrong moments were those
supporting David and not those from Romford.

Whenever I feel under pressure, I make sure I keep my head
down and don't move on the shot. Eventually, it paid off. I
took the important fifteenth frame to win the match 9–6, and
cheerfully collected the £10,000 cheque and the Yamaha
Organs trophy. At no time did it cross my mind that David
would overtake me, though I did wonder for a while if I'd ever
move off the figure eight.

If I had any thoughts of resting on my laurels after landing
this trophy, there was a shock in store. The following week was
the busiest of my life.

On 9 March I was to play Jim Meadowcroft in the first
round of the new John Courage English professional championships at the Haden Hill Leisure Centre in Birmingham.
On the morning of 10 March I was booked for an exhibition
match at the Deal Bowling Club in Kent. The ticket demand
was so big that the match had to be switched to the much
larger Sports Complex in Dover.

Still buzzing with the Yamaha success, I trounced Meadowcroft by nine games to two. Having disposed of him, I drove
out of Birmingham for Dover, having arranged to call at
Romford to pick up a driver.

In front of 750 people, the Dover show started promptly at
7.30, and after the exhibition frames and trick shots, I wasn't
back in Birmingham until five o'clock next morning. Desperate to put my head down, I stumbled into my hotel – only to
be told that my room had been taken because I was so late.
So there we were, my exhausted driver and I, down on our
knees at 5.30 in the morning, staggering around looking for
new accommodation. We eventually got to bed well past six.

In normal circumstances this wouldn't have mattered
much, but I was due to meet John Spencer in the quarter-
finals at 2.30 in the afternoon. John had been putting in a lot
of practice to improve his play. He was trying much harder all

round. His cue action was still not good, but he was definitely thinking about his game for a change.

John took the first frame, but I rallied well to lead 5–3 at the interval. The see-saw sequence continued, with John pulling out an absolute ace from the pack with a magnificent break of 112 to edge in front again by six games to five.

By now, I was so tired I was practically snoring on my feet. I was shattered. I kept drinking tea and coffee to keep myself awake. Without doubt, it was one of the most demanding games of my life. A towering test of stamina. I knew also, however, that to use tiredness as an excuse for my performance would be the easy way out, and an unsatisfactory one.

It was a ridiculous situation really, because in the twelfth frame, flat out on my feet, I pieced together a break of 138, the highest of the championship, to draw level at 6–6.

My whole game was revitalized. Suddenly, victory looked a definite possibility. With great determination I continued to keep my eyelids open and won the match by nine frames to seven.

There was hardly time to savour this gruelling win before I was out on the road again, this time heading south to Wantage in Oxfordshire for an evening's exhibition match. There was no let-up. Next day, it was back to London for yet another exhibition match, this time at Holborn on the Friday evening. My dad met me in the city and drove me through the night all the way back to Birmingham again. We arrived in the early hours of Saturday, which enabled me to have a good sleep before going out to play Ray Edmonds in the semi-final.

With my father driving me back like that, it reminded me of my amateur days when he shuttled me all over the country, sometimes arriving home at three in the morning, sleeping in a chair for a couple of hours, and then leaving for work at five.

In contrast to my match against Spencer, I met very little resistance from Ray Edmonds and, though the first four frames might have gone either way, I beat him 9–0.

Willie Thorne and Tony Meo met in the other semi-final,

and it was Tony who came off best by nine frames to eight after a titanic struggle.

In the final, Tony and I fought to find our rhythm. We gradually picked up as the game progressed and I'm convinced the match was decided in the fourth frame. Tony led 2–1 and just needed any easy yellow to leave me looking for snookers. But the yellow frustratingly rattled in the jaws and refused to drop for him. I stepped in, cleared the colours, and then potted the respotted black to level at 2–2.

From that moment, Tony crumbled. He began to cue badly, and I raced away with the match by nine frames to three. I definitely won that event playing well below the standard I had achieved in previous tournaments, and I was now more convinced than ever that to manage to win even when playing badly was the mark of a champion.

Again there was hardly time to order a round, let alone enjoy a drink, before I was flying off to Belfast to play Alex Higgins in a two-day match covering four sessions. I didn't even bother to go to bed. I drove straight from Birmingham and boarded the early-morning plane.

The Belfast match was again organized by the tireless Bob Kearney. He had hired the Ulster Hall – very much Alex's home venue. To some extent I had committed myself over this match in my column in the *Daily Star*. I wrote that I was going to Belfast to put my wares on the table, and that if I could beat Alex there, I could beat him anywhere.

Well, when you make statements like that, there are times when you can be left with your trousers round your ankles. I'm pleased to say that this was not one of those embarrassing occasions. I led 12–6 on the first day and eventually crushed him 19–7 with the fourth session left unplayed.

In the twenty-third frame I almost became the first player ever to make a 147 in a senior match in Ireland. Having sunk fifteen reds, fifteen blacks, the yellow and the green, I lost position on the brown. Nerves were entirely to blame. Nevertheless, the 125 delighted me no end, and everyone in the hall seemed thrilled with the attempt at the maximum break. Alex receives fanatical support in Belfast, but this was one occasion when his followers ended up cheering more for his opponent than they did for him. I was flattered. It was another break-through.

After Belfast, I flew back to Birmingham and drove on to Cheltenham for the Festival race meeting. I know nothing about horses, but Corals had asked me to present their trophy to the winner of their Golden Hurdle race which they sponsor every year.

I must confess I didn't fancy wasting a day watching a load of 'Dobbins' running around in circles, but once I reached the racecourse I enjoyed the social atmosphere. During the afternoon an optimistic BBC commentator asked me to select a horse for viewers, and I went for New Top as an each-way chance. It came in third at 16–1 – which, I suppose, wasn't bad for a beginner.

Barry, of course, did very much better. He came rushing back to say that a certain friendly trainer had tipped him a horse that had just won at 25–1. As a gambler, he's phenomenally lucky.

Meanwhile the Scots had also been crying out for a match between Alex and me. So on 23 March we met in front of a capacity crowd of 2,750 at the Kelvin Hall in Glasgow. This was the biggest audience I've ever played in front of – and hundreds more were locked outside. I shall never forget the deafening Hampden-type roar that greeted us. It certainly appealed to me. It spurred me on too, and I went out and beat Alex 5–3.

A place on Gareth Edwards's winning team on the BBC programme *Question of Sport* led up to a fascinating clash with Cliff Thorburn in an invitation challenge match down at the den in Romford.

We played on 28 March. It was my last serious contest before the world championships, and having seen the draw for the championships, I considered Thorburn the toughest of the players in my half. To have the chance to play him at Romford so close to the championships was a gift I grabbed with both hands. I beat him 6–0 and Barry hoped he'd remember it when we got to Sheffield.

The championships were barely a fortnight away, but I was determined not to relax in the nervous build-up to the world's most important tournament. I just wanted to keep busy, practising and playing exhibition matches. I wanted to forget about the championships and let them come along at their own steady pace.

12 Setting Up Camp

Finally, on 6 April 1981, I drove to Sheffield for what was to be a memorable campaign extending over an emotional and marvellous fortnight.

For a start, I knew that the winner would receive a cheque worth £20,000 – as much as Bjorn Borg earned for his last success at Wimbledon.

Of course, the reward for Embassy, the sponsors, comes mainly from enormous all-day television coverage. Sometimes, the cameras work practically without a break. From 11.30 in the morning until one o'clock next day. When the championships ended, as many as eighty hours of play had been transmitted. Not a frame was missed. Can you imagine a 147 being made in the first frame of a morning session and no one there to capture it live or on tape?

Such a disaster did occur once when John Spencer was playing in a sponsored tournament. John scored a magnificent 147, but the camera crew employed by an Independent Television company had tragically left the arena and gone for a tea break.

For me, the power of television is quite mind-boggling. Complete strangers suddenly feel they know me personally simply from seeing me on the box. It gives people a talking point, and helps to break the ice.

Television has worked a minor miracle for snooker. It has lifted the game from the pie-and-pint image to the best-suit brigade. It has turned billiard halls into snooker centres, and has made many of the top players rich men.

Though seeded number thirteen for the championships, a prize money table published at the time showed that I was topping the list with £32,000 to my name. This was virtually £8,000 more than the next man Alex Higgins, seeded number four. The top seed, Ray Reardon, was way down in fifth place, with a mere £15,300.

I put in a tremendous amount of hard work in preparing for the championships, including a few superstitious trips to Blackpool, where I played my good friend, Frank Callan. I had practised there during the United Kingdom championships, and as I won that tournament, I suppose it was only natural that I wanted to go back.

Cliff Thorburn was also there. Perhaps he's superstitious, too. He had practised there before the world championships the previous year, which, of course, he went on to win.

I remember lying awake at night thinking what it would be like to pot the last few balls in the final, and actually receive the cup for the first time. I would end up with tears rolling down my face at the thought of it. And I knew the same would happen if it really came true.

As the championships came closer my only worry concerned my cue. I knew the tip couldn't possibly last the whole competition, so I spent several anxious moments plucking up courage to cut it off and put on a new one. I did this just two days before the championships. As all snooker players know, a new tip needs a certain amount of 'playing in', and there was a chance that this could affect my performance, especially in the first-round match. I'm pleased to recall the tip turned out to be a good one.

Over the years, I had beaten all the top players at Romford, which I knew gave me a slight psychological edge even before the championships began. I was happy that, for one reason or another, I had the measure of all my opponents, and I was convinced that I had the ability, consistency and the all-important temperament to go out and beat them again. All I required was the opportunity to confirm it out there in the theatre where it mattered most.

The full extent of the public interest in the championships didn't really hit me until I was driving along the M1 to my Sheffield hotel on the evening before the first game, against Jimmy White. I heard a Corals advertisement on Radio Luxembourg announcing me as the 7–2 favourite to win the title.

A year before, I would have found it difficult to cope with being favourite. I would have kept looking over my shoulder for someone to beat me. But I had been favourite to win so many tournaments leading up to these championships, and had justified the forecasts so often, that I was no longer worried about being the main public fancy.

I knew my first game could be the most difficult as Jimmy was all the rage, and the player the Press were hailing as the new Alex Higgins. Jimmy turned professional after winning the world amateur title in Tasmania, and was regarded by many as the brightest prospect in snooker today. 'Whirlwind' White, as they call him, had received enormous publicity, and his clash with me had aroused tremendous interest and specu-lation. Jimmy, of course, had nothing to lose.

After the first session, I went to bed leading by four games to two, a sound performance, which included a 119 clearance. I had settled comfortably while Jimmy had displayed his lack of experience by attempting a number of low-percentage shots.

It was an identical story in the second session, which I again won 4–2, to put me 8–4 in front, and needing just two more frames for the match.

Barry was so confident that I had the game sewn up, he left Sheffield and drove back to London on business. He had just arrived in Romford when the amazing turn-around occurred. Barry heard the horror story while walking to his office. Stunned by the news, he dived into the first electrical store he could find and pleaded with the manager to switch on every television set he had on his shelves.

All of a sudden, my lead had slipped from 8–4 to 8–7, with Jimmy strutting around in top form. The alarm-bells were ringing. I was in real danger of seeing this year's chance slip through my fingers.

With time running out, I finally checked his onslaught with a vital break of seventy-four to breathe freely again at 9–7. But Jimmy still refused to surrender. Back he came to win the seventeenth frame, with the crowd roaring him on, cheering every shot he played, anxious to see the underdog pull off a surprise result.

Going into the eighteenth frame, I concentrated on keeping my head down. It worked. I withstood the pressure, struck a timely seventy-one break, and Jimmy finally capitulated, conceding the match on the yellow.

A duel that once looked a stroll in the park had become a scramble up a mountainside. I was glad to see it over. I left the arena and went straight for a chat with BBC commentator David Vine. I told him I found the table a lttle too fast, and that I had been forced to concentrate hard to keep Jimmy at bay. I also told him that I was glad that I had had such a hard game as it tuned me up for the much tougher battles ahead.

People keep telling me that concentration is one of my strong points. Strange really, because just about every school report complained that I 'did not pay enough attention' or that I was 'simply unable to apply himself'.

I'm dreadful when it comes to remembering names of people and things like that. But if it has anything to do with a challenge, then I can concentrate a hundred per cent for hours on end.

13 Being the Guv'nor

With Jimmy beaten, I now looked forward to facing Alex Higgins, a player with exactly the same aggressive attitude, and the type of opponent I definitely prefer to meet. A player of this sort always seems to present you with one extra opportunity to move in and win the frame.

Even before our game started, Alex went on television and tried a bit of psychology, claiming that he didn't 'fancy his chances a lot'. The bookmakers tended to agree with him, confidently marking me up as the 4–6 favourite.

Having already played one match in the arena, I obviously began with a slight advantage. I had acclimatized myself, whereas Alex was coming in stone cold.

All through the first session, he shook like a leaf. His trouser leg shook so badly it was quite visible, and it went on like that for several frames. In view of this perhaps it was not surprising that I reached the interval holding a commanding lead of six games to two.

Arriving back at the hotel, I relaxed for an hour or so on the three video machines that Barry and I had taken in. The hotel manager kindly allowed us to install them in a room on the tenth floor, almost next door to where I slept. Of the three machines, I usually played The Defender, the most sophisticated of its kind in the world. It had an emergency button labelled Smart Bomb which, when pressed, obliterates everything on the screen.

Alex picked himself up during the second session. He played

some excellent, attacking snooker and reduced the leeway to nine games to seven.

As the championships went on, it became more and more apparent that I was consistently winning the opening frame of each session. I had found I could settle in quickly. On setting off for the third session, Alex fluffed a red and I stepped in for a vital break of 45 to win yet another opener. Alex immediately struck back, but I was still enjoying the cushion of a two-frame lead and was never genuinely anxious. From 10–8 I pulled away, winning the next three frames to book a place in the quarter-finals against Terry Griffiths, who had disposed of Tony Meo with unexpected ease.

We were now at the end of the first week, and I remember sitting with Doug Mountjoy, and we both agreed how difficult it had become to eat a proper meal. I was living almost entirely on bacon sandwiches, grapefruits, and pints and pints of orange juice. I also found that I was taking my tension to bed with me. Usually, I can put my head on a pillow and collapse. Now I found it practically impossible to get the day's play out of my head, and it took me an eternity to get to sleep.

Terry demonstrated from the start that he was determined this was not going to be anything like the humiliating white-wash he suffered in the UK championships. I took the first frame, and he levelled immediately. By the end of the first session, nothing had dramatically changed. We were still all square at 4–4. Terry was playing exceptionally tight snooker and making me toil for every opening.

True to form, I again won the first frame of the next session. It proved an important boost, enabling me to press on and capture three games in a row. From my position I thought everything looked pretty good. Terry didn't entirely agree, hitting back to win the next game before I returned the compliment to win frame thirteen on the black and leave the scoreboard showing me ahead by eight frames to five.

Terry was playing infinitely better than at any time in the UK championships. He was cooler and much more careful.

Because of this, safety play became more and more an issue of the struggle, and the games got inordinately long.

By now, we were using up so much time that there was little chance of us finishing the eight frames permitted in the afternoon session. Queues were already forming outside the theatre for the evening match. I increased my lead to 9–5 before we were told the match had to come to a halt.

Resuming next day, Terry began with a brilliant break of one hundred to reduce the deficit to 9–6. I recovered straightaway to make it 10–6. Strangely, this was the score between us the previous year, only this time I wasn't looking over my shoulder for dangers.

Frame seventeen was a tense, cat-and-mouse affair which ended dramatically on the black. I tried to roll it along the top cushion towards the corner pocket, only to see it slow up to a stop and hang agonizingly on the lip. Terribly frustrated, I walked up and prodded it in with my cue, automatically conceding the game. I felt I should have potted that black, but I realized, too, that I had to shut it out of my mind or it could affect my play at a crucial stage in the game. There was nothing to be gained from looking back and kicking myself with regrets. I had to be positive. I had to keep my mind free and clear, and concentrate hard.

Thanks to some timely magic, I dominated the next frame and won it totally unchallenged by 133 to nil. Terry remained unperturbed and promptly tore back to win frame nineteen, making the scores 11–8, so the battle was still blazing.

The twentieth frame was one of those timeless affairs that looked as though it would never end. A gruelling, patient slog that lasted close on an hour. Concentration of the highest calibre was required, as neither of us would yield an inch. Eventually, and from nothing less than painstaking effort, the frame finally went my way, with a sigh, on the pink.

I knew just one more frame would be enough now to gain me a place in the semi-finals. But Terry just would not lie down. Another long, exhausting frame followed, and Terry pulled back to 12–9.

Though I needed only one frame, I still felt that if Terry could snatch one more himself he might start to think I was under some kind of pressure – and he wouldn't have been wrong!

The twenty-second frame started quietly enough, but then I sank a long red and set off on a match-winning break of fifty-two. For a moment, Terry again threatened to force his way back into contention, but the mountain was too steep to climb. At last I couldn't be caught, and I won an unforgettable match by thirteen frames to nine.

When interviewed by the Press, Terry told reporters, 'I thoroughly enjoyed that. When you play well and lose, it is not so important. It was a great game, with some fine snooker. I loved every minute of it.'

After he won the world championship, Terry was criticized in some quarters for playing too slowly. On reflection, I think this got to him by the end of his championship year, and he tried to speed up a bit. In doing do, it upset his rhythm and his play suffered. By the time we met in our momentous quarter-final, I think he had realized his mistake and reverted to his normal pace at the table. Judging by his performance, there was no doubt he had made the right decision.

Of course, with Terry out of the championships, I had now eliminated three world champions. Yet, there was still no relief. No sooner had I knocked one down, when up came another. Waiting to face me in the semi-final was the toughest of them all, defending world champion – and the grinder supreme – Cliff Thorburn.

I was pleased I had just played Terry, because he had tuned me up perfectly for Thorburn. The match was set over thirty-one frames, with the bookmakers unanimously listing me the 4–7 favourite. There was no doubt who the public thought would win.

I wish someone had told Thorburn. For once, I failed to

take the opening frame, but quickly compensated for the hiccup by taking the next three to lead 3–1 as we left the arena for a twenty-minute respite.

As you might expect, the packed theatre was hooked on every shot. One moment the whole place was applauding wildly, then the next it was as quiet as a graveyard.

I led 4–3 at the end of the first session, and was quite satisfied.

Because the draw had placed nearly all the top players in the same half, it seemed inevitable that the champion would ultimately come from this group. So in many ways, my match against Thorburn was as much a final as a semi-final.

Playing a lot of good snooker, I increased my lead to six games to four. Then, without warning, my whole world fell apart. My dreams became nightmares. Cliff completely froze me out, and he ended the session showing in front by eight games to six.

During this terrible part of the match, I went a full sixty-five minutes without potting a ball. I truly went to pieces. I have never been more pleased than when that session ended. If it had continued any longer, my chances could only have got worse. I couldn't leave The Crucible fast enough – just in case they called us back!

Some of the situations Cliff trapped me in during that spell were so awkward, I wished the table had a Smart Bomb button, as that seemed the only way out of trouble.

I marched straight for the hotel, furious with myself. Barry tried to keep up with me, but I didn't speak to him until we entered the lift. Then I said, 'I must be a mug.'

'Never mind,' he said, 'let's go upstairs and have a good laugh on the video.'

A marvellous idea. It was just what I needed. We went straight to The Defender and I played for an hour. Slowly, minute by minute, I could feel the tension and pressure gradually draining away from my system as I blasted all the little green Thorburns on the video screen. And I broke my record by hitting thirty-eight thousand of them! I played The Defender so often during the championships that when I went home I had a blister from pressing the buttons.

Slowly but surely, I cooled off. I felt relaxed and sent for sandwiches and a pot of tea. Then I took an hour's nap, had a bath, put on my dress-suit and said to Barry, 'Let's go to work. I want to play some snooker.'

On the walk back to the theatre for the evening session, Barry stopped me in the middle of Sheffield and said, 'Steve, if you're in front when we come back, I'll jump in that pool again.'

It's amazing how certain superstitions creep in during an event as important as the world championships. For instance, every time I walked to The Crucible, I deliberately stepped on a wooden cellar-lid on the pavement outside the Brown Bear pub; and by the end of the tournament everyone with me was being told to do the same – or the spell would be broken.

During the championships in the previous year, I always jumped over it, and as I was knocked out, Barry and I thought it was the lid that brought us bad luck. Silly really, but it is often little things like this that help to ease the tension. They tend to take my mind off the more serious matters of playing in a game.

Barry was always dreaming up new ideas to keep the fun flowing. Before that session against Thorburn, he was busy geeing everyone up, telling them that if they didn't need throat pastils by the end of the night, they would be sacked and sent home. He even told us he had kept the same pair of socks on for the whole championships, and had no intention of changing them until I had played my last game. I told him that this probably explained the strange smell in the video room.

Because I was always being shown as the favourite, sections of the crowd started to go against me and supported the underdog. Being an English lad, this hurt me. To emphasize how I felt, Barry went out and bought a large Union Jack, and he and the lads draped it over the balcony. Then they stood behind it and cheered like mad. On entering the theatre that night, the din was terrific. And just as I looked up and bowed to the Romford lads, they ceremoniously unrolled the flag for me and everyone else to see.

I came out for that session determined not to show the slightest emotion. During my spell on The Defender, cooling down, I realized where I had gone wrong. I had been expressing too much emotion, and consequently I had failed to live up to my nickname as The Romford Robot. By applying this attitude, I pulled myself together and, in one of the hardest sessions imaginable, powered my way past Thorburn to go in front by twelve games to ten.

At this point Thorburn, the great ice-cool grafter and normally a most affable man, unbelievably cracked. Because I held such a decisive lead at the end of the final frame of the evening, I put out my hand when I missed the pink, confident that Thorburn would see no point in carrying on, and would concede the frame without any fuss. If nothing else, it was around one o'clock in the morning, and I thought he would be as keen as me to get to bed.

To my great shock, Thorburn flatly refused to accept my hand, made as though to play the pink, stopped for a sip of water – obviously imitating me – and then finally conceded the frame. As we shook hands, he said, aggressively, 'I'll see you tomorrow!'

For anyone who wonders why I sip so much water during my matches, I find that the pressure of playing in top tournaments leaves my mouth dry and I feel uncomfortable. In certain atmospheres, my hands also tend to sweat badly and I spend a great deal of time drying them off and wiping the cue.

A short time after Thorburn's uncharacteristic outburst, he shocked me even more on our way back to the dressing-rooms. He accused me of being arrogant, and said, 'I've got more class in my arse.' I was so upset that I stormed out of The

Crucible without even waiting for Barry, and rushed back to the hotel on my own.

Thorburn had cracked in a way I never thought possible. What he said to me was overheard in the theatre and reported to John Williams, the senior tournament referee. Until then, I had always held the highest respect for Thorburn, both as a player and a man. I looked on him as the perfect professional. That is why this incident disappointed me so much. To be fair, he did try to put matters right a few days later when he came to my dressing-room and apologized, in front of Barry. He also went on television and apologized in public.

When a man of Thorburn's calibre snaps like that, it explains better than anything else all the pressures players have to suffer under the lights, in front of crowds and before the cameras.

Well, it wasn't all grim that night. Barry, as you'd expect, brightened up the proceedings when he entered the hotel all dripping wet, his new black shoes soaked from jumping in the pool as promised.

As for Thorburn, I vowed to beat him next day. If he had known me better, he would have hidden his feelings inside. I am not physically violent, but I channel it all in psyching myself up. I prefer to let the talking be done on the table. When David Vine asked me how I managed to recover so well against Thorburn, I told him, 'I scored thirty-eight thousand on The Defender.'

By now, in the second week of the championships, my fan-mail was bulging in three bags. Letters, telegrams and postcards had poured in to wish me luck and to congratulate me on my victories so far. One or two female admirers had even sent me the occasional red rose, and I was given enough Easter Eggs and cuddly bunnies to open a chocolate shop. Two girls, in particular, stood outside my dressing-room every day of the championships to wish me luck, and it is support like this which means so much to me.

All my fan-mail was kept in the office of Ken Smith, the

tournament's efficient liaison officer, who told me during the semi-final that I had gone well ahead in the Popularity Stakes. Yet, once again superstition got the better of me. I decided I would not read a word until the championships were over. It is not that the letters are ever offensive. Far from it. They are always warm, kind and complimentary. Some are funny, too, and a few are even kinky. One girl wrote suggestively that the 'only frame on my mind is yours. If I could get you on the table, you'd soon be asking for a rest!'

Hundreds and hundreds of people write asking for photographs, autographs and telephone numbers. In fact, the mail got so big during the championships and in the weeks that followed that I decided to set up a fan-club. The *Daily Star* has generously agreed to run it for me, and will send out regular newsletters to members and supply them with signed photographs and autographs whenever they are requested.

I was oozing confidence when I resumed at eleven o'clock in the morning against the belligerent Thorburn. I had slept well, and I was so deeply obsessed with the job in hand that the electrified atmosphere and the cheering went straight over my head. I played hard, methodical snooker. I ground him out of sight. He didn't win another frame. His 'see you tomorrow' threat had backfired on him. He lost his crown by a massive sixteen frames to ten.

When I looked up at my supporters on the balcony, standing and cheering madly, I was absolutely choked with emotion. I had made it to my first world final, and I had beaten the hardest man in the game to get there. There is no doubt that this was the toughest match of my whole career. I was proud to think that I had proved to everyone that I was hard enough to win the championship.

Stamina is one aspect of snooker that is all too commonly forgotten. Just because snooker players don't chase a football, or don't punch each other's brains out in a boxing-ring, it doesn't mean that we don't need to be in prime physical condition to do our best. I suppose there are one or two top players who might think that fitness is unimportant, believing they can best reach their peak by training on ten pints of beer a night, or by playing blackjack in a casino until four in the morning, but their form soon suffers. On many occasions, like the world championships in particular, a player can be on his feet for anything up to nine hours a day, performing under intense pressure, and lucky to receive a plate of sandwiches to keep him going.

Having said all this, you won't catch me jogging around the streets of Plumstead, chopping trees, or even doing a dozen press-ups a day. Equally, you won't see me sinking a gallon of beer every night, or staying out until the postman starts his round. At least not too often!

Fitness and stamina are a priority in these situations. There is also a major mental factor. The whole object is not to crack when the squeeze is applied. A lot of people, it seems, don't appreciate how imperative it is for players to keep their minds totally clear and alert when battling under extreme pressure. Being able to think clearly under pressure can make the difference between a good and bad match player.

Thorburn's view of our match was best summed up in the official report all players have to submit to the Association. This is what he wrote: '*Table:* Excellent. *Atmosphere:* How could it be better? *Lighting:* Adequate. *Referee:* Excellent. *General Report:* I don't like losing. *Signed,* Cliff Thorburn.'

Mum, Dad and Keith drove up through the night to watch my last session against Thorburn on the Saturday morning. I spoke to mum on the telephone on the Friday and asked her to bring a pair of brown shoes for me, as the ones I was wearing had broken – under the strain, no doubt.

During the championships I had taken a lot of leg-pulling from a number of friends who reckoned my light-blue suit was proving unlucky for me. They thought it should be sent to the cleaners and the ticket thrown away. They were convinced I played better in my browns. I usually replied by saying, 'Don't you remember, I won the UK title in my blue?'

To which they would say, 'But this isn't the UK, is it?'

I actually received several phone calls at The Crucible and in the hotel from people pleading with me to 'wear your lucky brown suit'. I don't really believe in things like that – and I'm not superstitious – but I wasn't keen on tempting fate! For my final, and memorable session against Thorburn, and for the rest of the championships, when not in evening dress, I always played – and won – in brown.

My family arrived just in time for the Thorburn game. I was actually leaving my hotel when they stumbled in, hungry and exhausted. Their car had broken down on the motorway, and dad and Keith had to push it on to a slip road. They finally left it at a garage and completed the journey by taxi.

Ray Martin, a milkman, and one of my best supporters, was in an even worse pickle. Hiss boss had told him that if he didn't return to Dartford straightaway, he would be sacked without notice. Not wanting to miss the final, Ray chose to travel to and from Dartford, a round trip of more than three hundred miles, three times in three days, never going to bed, but just catching a nap in the car at a service station.

By now I knew that Doug Mountjoy would be my opponent in the final. He had beaten his fellow-Welshman Ray Reardon, making a world record 145 break to earn himself a colossal £6,200 for just ten minutes' work. Watching the television highlights in bed that night, I caught a glimpse of Doug being interviewed. I quickly jumped out and turned down the sound, because I didn't want to hear what he had to say.

Barry, in the meantime, had dashed back to London to fetch Susan for the final, plus a magnum of champagne which he had been keeping cool in his garage for a month.

Not all the action in the championships had been confined to the table either. A blazing row had broken out over a decision by referee Jim Thorpe in a match involving Dennis Taylor and Kirk Stevens. Jim called Dennis for a push-shot on the blue. Little was said about it at the time, but Dennis later joked that it was not so much a push, but more like a shove! Sadly for Jim, and for everyone else connected with snooker, word leaked to the Press that promoter Mike Watterson had sacked the referee, and some nasty mud-slinging followed.

14 Reaching the Summit

The first frame of the thirty-five frame final was set to start at eleven o'clock on Easter Sunday morning. A Salvation Army band was parading through the deserted streets, and as it walked by, one of the trumpeters slowly lowered his instrument and wished me good luck. Yet another example of the wonderful support I received right through the championships.

So here, on 19 April 1981, the two days of reckoning had arrived. Soon I was to discover whether I had it in me or not. I believe to reach the pinnacle in any form of sport – to be a world champion – is not only a fantastic achievement, but also a great honour. You commit your whole life to one particular sport, enduring endless hours of practice, frustration, loneliness and self-discipline, and to reach the summit is the ultimate reward.

Now, I was just one match away from being world champion. Just think, the *best snooker player on Earth!* It scared me a bit. To come this far and lose would be unbearable.

Every time the thought of being champion crossed my mind, I tried to think hard of something else. I had to keep my mind clear. Just another game, I told myself. Even so, I knew that if I won, it would prove too much for me. I had to control my emotions until then.

Doug is a devastating potter of a ball. A grafter. A player who works hard for his openings. I knew full well I couldn't afford to leave the balls lying around for him to swoop on. He can be lethal. On the debit side, I knew Doug made no claim to be the best positional player in the world; but then, when you can pot a ball like him, who needs perfect position? Doug was seeded number fourteen, one below me. He had long since proved his strength by winning the world amateur championship in 1976, followed by the tough Benson and Hedges Masters the next year, immediately after turning professional. He then went on and won the 1978 Coral UK title.

Again the bookmakers had marked me up as favourite. This time at the ridiculous odds of 1–3, with Doug at 5–2, although Doug did attract a great deal of support just before the match got under way.

I couldn't recall losing to Doug since my early days at Romford, apart from that one-frame defeat in Pot Black. All things being equal, I thought I had every right to feel confident.

For some time leading up to the championships, Doug had suffered from a nasty nervous complaint called Bell's Palsy. This affected the muscles on the left side of his face to such an extent that it troubled his vision. Fortunately for him, the problem had virtually cleared up by the time the championships came around and Doug was back to his best.

So the final was upon us. While warming up on the practice table, some fifteen minutes before entering the arena, I could hear David Vine, sitting the other side of a curtain, introducing the day's television broadcast and running through the records of each player. I could hear him clearly introducing me as the 'ice-cool Steve Davis'. Unknown to him, I was just a few yards away, shaking like a leaf, hardly able to pot a ball, and wondering whether I should visit the toilet just once more.

We were both introduced in the arena and the photographers swarmed around us to take pictures with the cup for what seemed an eternity. Doug amused the crowd by pretending to polish it. Superstitiously, I decided I wouldn't touch it until the trophy was rightfully mine.

Finally the photographers dispersed, and we were able to get on with the game . . .

I raced off with a fifty-nine break to cancel out a forty from Doug and capture the all-important first frame, Doug conceding on the pink. My cueing felt just right, and I slipped into a nice, relaxed mood straightaway. A fifty-two break in the second frame put me two–nil up, the game ending 81–38.

Breaks of twenty-four and forty-nine won me the third frame by an overwhelming 80–7, and breaks of thirty-four and thirty gave me the fourth frame by an even bigger margin of 81–1, Doug conceding with two reds still left on the table.

Trailing four–nil, Doug's game was in total disarray. He kept lifting his head on the shot and was visibly distressed at missing his opportunities.

The same flowing pattern continued in the fifth frame. A break of fifty-two sent me racing clear to win 92–14. The sixth frame followed in identical fashion, and the final was swiftly developing into a crazy, one-sided anti-climax. I was playing really great snooker, and thriving in the atmosphere of the arena. It was a tremendous feeling to know that I was playing so well on such an important day.

Then, when least expected, the routine changed. In a scrappy frame the blue and black became wedged in the jaws of the bottom corner pocket. Neither Doug nor I could dare risk knocking the black in, so referee John Williams, realizing we had reached stalemate, decided there was no alternative but to pick up the balls and restart the frame.

On reflection, I think this gave Doug a chance to get his rhythm going. He won the replayed frame, and so brought my rampage to a sudden halt. With nothing to lose, he then rammed in a break of seventy-six to win the eighth frame by 110–9. Not content with this, he kept up the pounding to take the ninth frame 70–2. The Welsh contingent welcomed the recovery, bursting into long and loud cheering, clearly relieved that the fight was not over.

From dominating the match 6–0, by the end of the first session I had plunged to 6–3. Doug had come back from the dead. Despite all this, I kept telling myself that I was battling for the world title. To hold a three-frame lead at that stage was a tremendous advantage.

Owing to the replayed frame, the session didn't end until 6.45. According to the schedule, we were expected back at the table, all freshly changed into evening attire, by 7.30, so I set off in a frantic dash to the hotel to smarten up.

Doug and I were both staying at a hotel about ten minutes' walk away. There certainly was no time for a proper meal, and hardly enough for a cup of tea. I dived under the shower, slipped into my evening suit, rushed through one 'superstitious' game on The Defender, picked up my cue and hurried to the lift with mum, dad, Keith, Barry, Susan and a few lads from Romford just behind. As the doors opened, a waiter came along with a tray of sandwiches, and we ambushed him and ate them ravenously as we travelled down to the ground floor.

Darting from the hotel, there were barely fifteen minutes left in which to reach The Crucible. I clicked into gear straightaway and took the first frame 81–28. A right nailbiter came next, with Doug recovering well to nick the frame by the narrowest of margins, 62–61, after sinking both the pink and the black. He kept up this exhilarating fightback in frame twelve, again winning narrowly by 57–47.

Frame thirteen proved lucky for me. I outplayed him 73–24. Then Doug unleashed one of his tremendous potting assaults to build a magnificent break of 129, without me offering a single reply. A whitewash. It happens to us all! In a mood of 'anything you can do, I can do better' I hit straight back with a break of eighty-one to clinch frame fifteen 89–9.

Compared with the earlier drama, the next two frames were dull and mediocre, sprinkled with only a few small breaks. Doug won the sixteenth, and I took the next.

With one frame remaining on the first day, I knew I could leave the theatre leading either by four frames or by two. I soon had the answer. Doug dashed off with a break of thirty-three, I countered with one of thirty-two, but he took control

again, potting the balls that mattered to win the applause with
a score of 98–49. So going to bed after the first day, I led by
ten games to eight – too close for a good night's sleep.

Waking up next morning, I was hardly able to eat breakfast
at all. The only food I coud stomach were four halves of
grapefruit.

In starting the third session, I promptly produced a break
of eighty-three which pleased me a lot. It impressed John
Spencer, too. John was giving expert advice in the commentator's box, and he told viewers he couldn't believe how well I
kept starting my sessions.

I captured the frame 112–15 to go three in front again.
Frame twenty was much the same. This time 81–34. But Doug
refused to put away his cue and surrender, creating a break of
forty-two to win frame twenty-one by 71–29. Doug maintained the momentum in the following frame, piercing together a fine break of sixty-eight from an excellent opening red
to win 86–50. So, after all this time, just two frames were
keeping us apart.

The tense cliffhangers continued. I retaliated with a break
of fifty-four to win frame twenty-three by 102–9, but Doug
responded yet again with a break of forty-four to take the next
one by 75–15. After being six-nil in front, I was now finding
it desperately difficult to shake off my man, leading him now
by 13–11.

I could quite understand my supporters becoming more
and more anxious as the frames went by, but I gave them
plenty to cheer in frame twenty-five. Doug began impressively
with a splendid break of forty-six, but I replied immediately
with one of fifty-five, just to let Romford know that I hadn't
fallen asleep. This frame was crucial to both of us, and was
settled finally – and for Doug, tragically – on the blue. Doug
potted the ball all right, but before he had time to smile his
pleasure, the white ball had trickled in-off. This presented me
with the blue off its spot, and I took it and squeezed home by
75–69.

With frame twenty-six approaching, I was back in the position I found myself in before breaking off at the end of the previous session: after it I would be leading either by four or by two.

Each frame was becoming more and more important. Doug stayed firmly on the defensive until a superb shot on the blue saw the cue-ball nudge the pink off the cushion. With the frame at his mercy, Doug carried on to pot the black and win 57–49. So the morning session on the final day ended with me still clinging on to my two-nil lead.

Before returning for the vital finale, I tried to relax by eating a meal, which I followed with a further session on The Defender. Ominously for Doug, I clocked up forty-six thousand. Though just a short time away from the most important hours of my career, I told the Press I was relaxed and confident. I felt terrible!

The final session was beamed live to seventeen million viewers, and the theatre itself was jam-packed, with not a spare seat in sight. Touts had enjoyed a brisk trade outside, pocketing up to fifty pounds for five-pound tickets.

Behind the scenes a camera crew were busy covering the route Doug and I were taking from our dressing-rooms to the gladiator pit. We couldn't even be nervous in private, but it worked well for television. David Vine came up and asked me how I felt. I tried to relax, and said that I was going to treat it as just another game of snooker.

After trailing six–nil, Doug couldn't have dreamt of being just two down going into the final session. Yet he knew he had to make an impression quickly. He knew he had to remove the deficit in the same way as I had done in the semi-final against Thorburn. But once again my ability to settle straightaway into a smooth rhythm soon cut short any charge he might have had in mind, and when Doug missed a long red, I was straight into my stride, constructing a good break of eighty-four to win frame twenty-seven by 100–32.

A clearance of 119 brought me frame twenty-eight, and when a break of forty-four clinched the twenty-ninth, I needed just one more frame to tie up the championship. I was playing better than at any time during the tournament, even allowing for the top quality snooker I achieved during the first six frames of the final.

By now, Doug was understandably demoralized.

Barry had already asked me during the day whether we should meet again in the dressing-room to discuss my speech. I told him he must be kidding. I had played the championships over and over again in my mind for the past twelve months, and I knew exactly what I was going to say.

After a comedy of errors in frame thirty, with me suffering a bout of almost-there nerves, I finally put together a break of forty-nine. I potted the green, and a glance at the scoreboard told me I needed the brown along the bottom cushion to be safe. It went in like a dream, and all of a sudden it hit me that I had done it. From the moment I potted the blue and scrambled in the pink, I felt the tears welling up inside me. I had won 18–12, and the world title was mine.

The whole place erupted. I was so overcome by emotion that I shut my eyes in disbelief. Few people can realize the type of pressure Doug and I had lived through during those championships. We shook hands, and I remember thinking how terrible it must be to lose in a world championship final.

Then I saw Barry charging towards me, teeth clenched, fist clenched. I knew just how he felt. We had dreamt of this moment for so long. He hit me like a tank, grabbing me hard around the shoulders, and almost knocking me to the ground. I remember thinking I was lucky to have such a good stance.

Then I saw my father, and all I remember him saying was, 'That was good snooker, son.' When I saw the pleasure on his face, I knew what it meant to him. We had worked hard and come a long way. We hugged each other until dad decided this wasn't the role he had imagined for his first television appearance. By now tears were flowing down my cheeks, and I was really glad when Susan came along and gave me an excuse for a proper hug.

I ask you, there I was at the top of the world, and I couldn't laugh for crying. Mum had meanwhile satisfied herself with a 'well done' touch on my shoulder, as well as having a nice big kiss from dad in the background.

David Vine appeared again as the chaos subsided and he promptly confirmed the magic moment by announcing 'Steve Davis, world snooker champion 1981'. Still stunned by my win, the din and the flood of congratulations, I finally said to him. 'Oh, Jesus Christ...' I was exhausted. For weeks after the championships, even though I won, I couldn't have faced the task all over again. I was drained, both physically and mentally.

He then asked me what in the circumstances amounted to nothing less than a string of Mastermind questions, until he left me alone and gave Doug the same Magnus Magnusson grilling.

This whole interview is on video, and I play it time and time again, never tiring of watching it.

Mr Christopher Cory, managing-director of Wills, the sponsors, arrived like a man from Securicor, and presented Doug with a cheque for £16,200 – which couldn't be bad. He pocketed a further £10,000 for finishing runner-up; £1,200 for the highest break; and a further £5,000 for setting a new championship record with that magnificent break of 145.

Then came my turn – a cheque for £20,000, and my reward, the most famous trophy in the game. I again held it high, showing it off to my family and friends, and as the army of photographers clicked away, my head began to clear. I was ready to make a speech. I thanked everyone who had helped to make the championships such a great success, plus all my well-wishers and then, on a personal note, eventually got round to the most important part of what I had to say – which was to thank my mum and dad, and Barry and Susan, for everything.

My brother, Keith, and my girlfriend, Helen, were also very much in my thoughts. Unfortunately for both of us, Helen was not able to be there, but immediately the fuss had died down, I spoke to her on the telephone. She was as happy as the rest of us.

With the speeches over, the cameras switched off, the table being dismantled, and the chattering crowds leaving in their droves, it was time to find a suitable place to uncork Barry's bottle of champagne.

The Press lads were magnificent and came to our rescue. They readily opened the doors to their large room, where the typewriters were rattling and the telephones ringing, and allowed me to go in and celebrate as privately as possible with my family and friends. They also let in the whole Romford Roar, so all the stories that were written that evening for next day's papers were done to a rowdy background of singing, drinking and cheering.

There has never been a day like it for any of us. While I was sipping champagne with dad, he casually put a hand in his pocket and brought out a fistful of pound notes. The story then came out that during an interval at The Crucible, a friend of dad's had told him that a horse called Aldenham was racing at Kempton that afternoon. As Aldenham is the depot where dad works, he decided to risk a pound on the nag. As a rule, dad never bets. I'm not so sure that he even knows how to write out the slip. In this case, the friend did it for him – and the horse won at 25–1!

Barry did even better. When our party broke up in the Pressroom, eight of us, all family and friends, went off to the Napoleon Casino in Sheffield to enjoy the best meal for miles. While waiting for the first course to be served, Barry nipped outside to try his luck on the roulette-wheel, and rushed back, beaming, with £650 worth of chips filling his hands! He had put the whole on number nineteen and had hit the jackpot. It was just that type of day.

The funniest incident occurred while walking back to my hotel with the trophy shining in my arms. On reaching the 'lucky' pub cellar-lid, I put my cue against the wall and got down on my hands and knees and gave the old, battered door a great big kiss. It didn't taste too nice, but I thought it deserved a little show of gratitude.

While down on all fours, I didn't notice that a police officer was standing on the corner across the road, staring at this strange, ginger-haired fellow in evening dress kissing a mucky door in the middle of Sheffield. As I got to my feet, he looked over at me, grinned and walking away, not bothering to ask for my autograph, or even to lock me up for the night!

There are many, many wonderful reasons why 19 April 1981 is a day I shall never forget. In fact, I can't imagine another year like it.

All through my career, my dad and Barry have sat together watching me playing in my big matches. They rabbit on like two old women, trying to predict my next shot, and invariably get it wrong. One day I intend to put a tape-recorder under their seats and find out exactly what they talk about. During the celebrations that followed the world championships, they both shook hands and said 'Well played' to each other. I certainly wasn't going to argue.

Having secured the world title, it meant that I had won five major events in five months for a total of £45,000 in prize-money. When I left The Crucible for the last time, I had played sixty-seven days in a row without a night off. And in the world championships alone I had played 146 frames. I really needed a rest, but I didn't get one until three months later when I relaxed on a fabulous sunshine cruise to the Caribbean.

Right through my playing career, it has been my ambition to be the world champion, and also to be the best player in the world. The two are not always the same, though in my case I should like to think they are.

I am proud to be the champion of the world. It's the greatest honour possible. I am truly grateful to everyone who has helped me make it to the top.

My next ambition is to stay there.

Appendix A
Steve Davis's Playing Career

1971
Began playing snooker seriously.

January 2nd: First 100 break (102) at Plumstead Workingmen's club.

Southern Area Snooker Champion.

Runner-up Southern Area Junior Billiards Championship.

1976
Southern Area Junior Champion.

Losing semi-finalist British Junior Snooker Championship – lost to Ian Williamson.

British Junior Billiards Champion – beat Ian Williamson.

September Lucania National Snooker Championship finalist – lost to Geoff Foulds.

November Lucania National Tour with Geoff Foulds and Russell Jarmak.

1977
London and Home Counties Billiards Champion.

January Wandsworth Classic Champion.

August 2nd: First 147 maximum break at
Plumstead Common Workingmen's club.

September London and Home Counties Jubilee
Champion – beat Vic Harris in the final.

Lucania Pro-Am Champion – beat Ray
Reardon, Russell Jarmak and Geoff Foulds.

Lucania National Champion – beat Russell Jarmak.

December Challenge match at Romford – beat
John Spencer 5–1.

Northern Snooker Centre (Leeds)
quarter-final – beat Ray Reardon 5–3.

Northern Snooker Centre (Leeds) semi-final –
beat Fred Davis 5–0.

1978
January Northern Snooker Centre (Leeds) final –
beat John Virgo 8–3.

Qualified for English Snooker Championship
final southern section.

February 17th: First English Amateur International
match versus Scotland at Doncaster.

Challenge match at Romford – beat
Alex Higgins 5–3.

English Snooker Amateur Championship –
lost to Mike Hallett 4–2 (quarter-final).

March Second appearance for England versus
Wales at Cardiff.

April CIU Billiards Championship – semi-final –
beat Dave Burgess.

May   Pontins Open Champion – beat Tony Meo 7–6.

Losing semi-finalist in Canadian Club Invitation Snooker Handicap.

Losing semi-finalist in Warners Open – lost to Tony Knowles.

Challenge match at Romford – lost to Doug Mountjoy 5–2.

Lucania National tour with Russell Jarmak.

June   CIU Snooker Championship – semi-final – beat Alwyn Lloyd 4–2.

Unbeaten Lucania team won British team championship (Blackpool).

Challenge match at Romford – beat Patsy Fagan 5–1.

July   CIU Snooker champion – beat Jack Fitzmaurice 4–2 in final.

CIU Billiards final – lost to Norman Dagley.

August   Canadian Open (Toronto) – lost to Alex Higgins 9–8 (quarter-final).

Lucania Pro-Am Champion – beat Vic Harris 5–1 in final.

17th: Accepted as professional snooker player by the WPBSA.

November   Challenge match at Romford – beat Cliff Wilson 5–4.

December   Challenge match at Romford – beat Ray Reardon 14–11.

First Pot Black TV appearance.

1979

January	Castle Club Pro-Am – lost to Cliff Thorburn 4–3.
February	UK Billiards Championship (Leeds) – lost to John Barrie.
	Demmy Pro-Am final (Manchester) – lost to John Virgo 5–0.
	Tolly Cobbold (Suffolk) Championship – first Professional Tournament.
March	Challenge match at Romford – beat Alex Higgins 33–23.
	Coral sponsored tour with Fred Davis.
April	World Snooker Championship – preliminary round – beat Ian Anderson 9–1.
	World Championship – qualifying round – beat Patsy Fagan 9–2.
	World Championship (Sheffield) – first round – lost to Dennis Taylor 13–11.
May	Pontins Open Champion – beat Jimmy White (Rec. 30) 7–3.
	Pro-Celebrity TV tournament (Leeds) partnered Ronnie Dukes.
June	Lucania Pro-Am quarter-final – beat Graham Miles 5–3.
July	North Ormsby Invitation Champion – beat Cliff Wilson 4–3 in final.
August	Canadian Open Championship – lost to Cliff Thorburn 9–6.
September	147 maximum break at Commonwealth Sporting Club (Blackpool).

October   Lucania Pro-Am semi-final – beat
             Doug Mountjoy 5–1.

November   Challenge match at Romford – beat
             Terry Griffiths 13–2.

             UK Snooker Championship (Preston)

             Beat: John Dunning 9–2 (first round)
                   Doug Mountjoy 9–6 (second round)

             Lost to: John Virgo 9–6 (quarter-final).

December   Indian Open (Bombay) lost to Cliff
             Thorburn in semi-final.

             1980

January   *1st:* 147 maximum break at Plumstead
             Common Workingmen's club.

             Lucania Pro-Am Championship – beat
             Dennis Taylor 8–0 in final.

             British Gold Cup – lost to Tony Meo
             (qualifying group).

             Louth Pro-Am tournament – beat Jimmy
             White 6–5 in semi-final.

February   Challenge match at Romford – beat
             Eddie Charlton 5–1.

             Challenge match at Romford – beat
             Cliff Thorburn 8–6.

             Challenge match at Romford – beat
             Perrie Mans 5–3.

             UK Billiards Championship – lost to
             Rex Williams (quarter-final).

             Louth Pro-Am tournament – beat Tony Meo
             8–3 in final.

Demmy Pro-Am final (Manchester) lost to
Jimmy White 5–3.

April World Championship – qualifying round –
beat Chris Ross 9–2.

World Championship – qualifying round –
beat Paddy Morgan 9–0.

World Championship (Sheffield)

Beat: Patsy Fagan 10–6 (first round)
      Terry Griffiths 13–10 (second round)
Lost to: Alex Higgins 13–9 (quarter-final).

May Warners Open Champion – beat
Brian Watson (Rec. 21) 5–1 in final.

June Lucania Pro-Am Championship – lost to
Tony Meo 5–1.

July Pro-Celebrity tournament (Leeds) –
partnered Dave Lee Travis.

August Canadian Open tournament – lost to
Terry Griffiths 9–2 (quarter-final).

October Champion of Champions tournament (London).

Beat Dennis Taylor 5–4, Kirk Stevens 7–2;
lost to John Virgo 4–5; beat Ray Reardon 5–4;
finished second in group.

November World Billiards Championship – lost to
John Barrie (quarter-final).

UK Snooker Championship (Preston)

Beat: Mike Hallett 9–1 (first round)
      Bill Werbeniuk 9–3 (second round)
      Tony Meo 9–5 (quarter-final)
      Terry Griffiths 9–0 (semi-final)
      Alex Higgins 16–6 (final).

December Won Wilson's Classic tournament – beat
Dennis Taylor 4–2 in final.

Pot Black TV.

1981

January Benson & Hedges Masters (London) – first
round – lost to Perrie Mans 5–3.

February UK Billiards Championship – lost to
Rex Williams (quarter-final).

Benson & Hedges Irish Masters – lost to
Ray Reardon 5–2 (quarter-final).

March Won Yamaha Organs Trophy – beat David
Taylor 9–6 in final.

John Courage English Snooker Championship –
beat Tony Meo 9–3 in final.

Challenge match at Romford – beat
Cliff Thorburn 6–0.

April World Championship (Sheffield)

Beat: Jimmy White 10–8 (first round)
       Alex Higgins 13–8 (second round)
       Terry Griffiths 13–9 (quarter-final)
       Cliff Thorburn 16–10 (semi-final)
       Doug Mountjoy 18–12 (final).

May Won Guinness Open (Isle of Wight) – beat
Mike Darrington.

September Jamieson International Masters - beat
Dennis Taylor 9–0.

October Captained England to victory in the State
Express World Team Championship – England
beat Wales in the final 7–6.

November Coral UK Professional Snooker Championship –
beat Terry Griffiths 16–3.

1982

January Recorded first TV 147 maximum break in
the Lada Classic – lost to Terry Griffiths
9–8 in final.

Won Pot Black TV – beat Eddie Charlton 2–0 in
final.

Benson & Hedges Masters – beat
Terry Griffiths 9–6 in final.

February Won Tolly Cobbold invitation Snooker
Championship (Ipswich) – beat Dennis Taylor
9–3 in final.

March Won Yamaha Organs Trophy – beat
Terry Griffiths 9–7 in final.

Benson & Hedges Irish Masters – lost to
Terry Griffiths 9–5.

April World Championship – first round – lost to
Tony Knowles 10–1.

May Pontins Professional tournament – beat
Ray Reardon 9–4.

Appendix B

*Frame-by-frame record of the 1981
World Professional Snooker
Championships*

(figures in brackets indicate breaks of fifty and over)

First round: Steve Davis v. Jimmy White

Played on 7, 8, 9 April over the best of 19 frames

Frame Number	Steve Davis	Jimmy White
1	72	20
2	68	22
3	46	70
4	90	1
5	124 (119)	8
6	36	65
7	36	71
8	64	50
9	47	57
10	138 (106)	0
11	98	85
12	70 (55)	13
13	28	76
14	55	73
15	67	73 (50)
16	74 (56)	0
17	21	85
18	89 (71)	17

Steve Davis 10 – Jimmy White 8

Second round: Steve Davis v. Alex Higgins

Played on 10, 11, 12 April over the best of 25 frames

Frame Number	Steve Davis	Alex Higgins
1	86 (78)	24
2	74	28
3	45	61
4	81 (61)	17
5	91 (69)	29
6	70 (63)	61
7	22	71
8	60	30
9	68	77
10	60	5
11	11	94
12	17	87
13	75	47
14	65	23
15	18	70
16	36	59
17	77	48
18	34	72 (52)
19	80 (73)	14
20	88	15
21	65 (51)	21

Steve Davis 13 – Alex Higgins 8

Quarter-final: Steve Davis v. Terry Griffiths

Played on 13, 14, 15 April over the best of 25 frames

Frame Number	Steve Davis	Terry Griffiths
1	59	39
2	38	81
3	83	6
4	75	10
5	44	84
6	61	34
7	14	74
8	58	83
9	59	46
10	82 (67)	37
11	73	59
12	11	67
13	66	52
14	87	14
15	6	120 (100)
16	87 (58)	21
17	50	54
18	133 (71)	0
19	29	81 (54)
20	60	49
21	15	73
22	69 (52)	43

Steve Davis 13 – Terry Griffiths 9

Semi-final: Steve Davis v. Cliff Thorburn

Played on 16, 17, 18 April over the best of 31 frames

Frame Number	Steve Davis	Cliff Thorburn
1	22	92
2	79	41
3	62	43
4	85 (51)	26
5	45	73
6	11	71
7	66	54 (54)
8	53	11
9	34	56
10	52	38
11	0	67
12	4	123 (91)
13	6	79
14	25	78
15	61	46
16	77	40
17	56	67
18	59	46
19	111 (59)	15
20	57	46
21	42	81
22	80	23
23	65	42
24	96 (50)	22
25	82	39
26	60	49

Steve Davis 16 – Cliff Thorburn 10

Final: Steve Davis v. Doug Mountjoy

Played on 19, 20 April over the best of 35 frames

Frame Number	Steve Davis	Doug Mountjoy
1	74 (59)	40
2	81 (52)	38
3	80	7
4	81	1
5	92 (56)	14
6	93	0
7	44	77
8	9	110 (76)
9	2	70
10	81	28
11	61	62
12	47	57
13	73	24
14	0	129 (129)
15	89 (81)	9
16	39	63
17	69	43
18	49	98
19	112 (83)	15
20	81	34
21	29	79
22	30	86 (68)
23	102 (54)	9
24	15	75
25	79 (55)	60
26	49	57
27	100 (84)	32
28	119 (119)	8
29	62	30
30	73	36

Steve Davis 18 – Doug Mountjoy 12

Dick Francis
The Sport of Queens £1.50

Dick Francis' autobiography, which provides fascinating and vivid insights into the owners, trainers, jockeys and horses that make up the thrilling 'sport of queens'. First published in 1957, this edition has been fully revised and brought up to date by the author.

'Sheer enchantment' SPORTING CHRONICLE

Alan Stewart
Birdman £1.50

One man's story of his extraordinary obsession – to fly free as a bird under his own power. For years Alan Stewart has been constructing muscle-powered flying machines in garages and garden sheds, financing his dream on a shoe-string. At forty-nine he is beginning the last lap – finally sure that he's found the way to beat gravity with a set of human limbs.

'A spiritual descendant of the birdmen, the tower jumpers, the cliff leapers of old, who used to step boldly into thin air to pit their wings against gravity and paid the price' OBSERVER

Desmond Wilcox and Esther Rantzen
Kill the Chocolate Biscuit £1.50
or behind the screen

The studio director was having trouble with a two-line sketch about cheating on a diet:
    'Is the chocolate biscuit dead?'
    'Yes.'
    'Right, kill the chocolate biscuit!'
    Moments like this, say Desmond Wilcox and Esther Rantzen, can 'sum up the lunatic nature of the world in which we earn our living!' Here's the truth about the extraordinary labyrinth behind the TV screen, told by two of the biggest names appearing in front of the camera.

Gerald Abrahams
The Pan Book of Chess £1.50

Starting – for the benefit of the complete tyro – with the basic moves
and rules of chess, the author goes on to describe the subtle features
of the game. The book initiates the beginner into methods of exploiting
the 'fork', the 'pin', etc, demonstrates tactics and strategy, shows how
battles are won – or lost – and examines and analyses openings and
endgames. Throughout, the author illustrates his lessons with
examples from actual play, including many brilliant games by the
masters.

Hubert Phillips
The Pan Book of Card Games £1.75

No other book of card games explains so many games so thoroughly
or offers so much instruction. The late Hubert Phillips, first chairman of
the English Bridge Union, was long recognized as Britain's leading
authority on card games. This famous work, with its clear descriptions
and its innumerable specimen hands played out card by card, will
afford every reader hours of entertainment.

'This fine book describes all the best of the old games and several new
ones' OBSERVER

'Hubert Phillips describes most lucidly fifty card games and more than
twenty-five games of Patience' SUNDAY TIMES

Oswald Jacoby and John Crawford
The Backgammon Book £2.50

A complete, up-to-date, step-by-step guide on how to play
backgammon for love or money – and win. Written by two world
champions and illustrated with large, precise diagrams, this essential
guide ranges from the crucial opening moves to the finer points of the
middle and end games. In addition to probability tables, etiquette and
the official rules of the International Backgammon Association, there
are chapters on the history of the game, how to run a tournament and
how to play chouette (backgammon for more than two people) plus a
useful glossary.

David Barber
We Won the Cup £1.75

'This year will see the one hundredth Football Association Challenge
Cup Final played. This book has been written to mark the occasion.
We Won the Cup contains a report on each of the ninety-nine Cup
Finals played since 1872, illustrated with photographs of some of the
most memorable moments from those matches . . .' TED CROKER –
SECRETARY OF THE FA

Michael Raper and Graham Sharpe
The Racing Ready Reckoner 80p

The essential book for every punter's pocket. To win or for a place –
whatever the stake, whatever the odds – *The Racing Ready Reckoner*
will work out your winnings in less time than it takes to fill out a
betting slip.

Terence Reese and Albert Dormer
Bridge: The ACOL System of Bidding 80p

ACOL is the bidding system used by eight out of every ten bridge
players. Written by two top level tournament players and packed with
examples and practical explanation here is *the* guide to making the
ACOL system give a new winning streak to your game.

Maxine Brady
The Monopoly Book £1.25

This book tells you how the world's most popular game started, where
it is played, the folklore surrounding it; the rules – the basic object of
the game, general clarification of some often misused rules: strategy
and tactics – outwit opponents with ruses like the 'pauper's attack', the
'bidder's delight' and the 'station offensive'. With a delightful epilogue,
'How to deal with tantrums', here is a comprehensive, illustrated and
entertaining compendium for Monopoly enthusiasts.

Ralph Denyer
The Guitar Handbook £5.95

A complete guide to playing the guitar – from simple chords to
advanced improvisation – with photographs, drawings and charts plus
a Chord Dictionary with more than 800 easy-to-follow fingerings.
Chapters on guitar and equipment maintenance and repair,
customizing your own instrument and recording your own music.

Jonathon Green
A Dictionary of Contemporary Quotations
£2.50

'Words are all we have' – Samuel Beckett; wise words, witty words,
weird words, all from the mouths of the famous and fashionable of
the last four decades – seven thousand quotations from prophets and
punks, movie scripts and millionaires, just about everyone from
Wittgenstein to Ernie Wise.

Barty Phillips
The Bargain Book £1.95

There are a thousand-and-one ways to pay less if you know where to
go and how to go about it. Packed with shrewd advice and lots of
addresses, from clothing to camping equipment, insurance to incense,
rugmaking to records, here's the handbook for everyone who loves a
bargain.

Fiction

☐ **Options**	Freda Bright	£1.50p
☐ **The Thirty-nine Steps**	John Buchan	£1.50p
☐ **Secret of Blackoaks**	Ashley Carter	£1.50p
☐ **Winged Victory**	Barbara Cartland	95p
☐ **The Sittaford Mystery**	Agatha Christie	£1.00p
☐ **Dupe**	Liza Cody	£1.25p
☐ **Lovers and Gamblers**	Jackie Collins	£2.25p
☐ **Sphinx**	Robin Cook	£1.25p
☐ **Ragtime**	E. L. Doctorow	£1.50p
☐ **Rebecca**	Daphne du Maurier	£1.75p
☐ **Flashman**	George Macdonald Fraser	£1.50p
☐ **The Moneychangers**	Arthur Hailey	£1.95p
☐ **Secrets**	Unity Hall	£1.50p
☐ **Simon the Coldheart**	Georgette Heyer	95p
☐ **The Eagle Has Landed**	Jack Higgins	£1.75p
☐ **The Master Sniper**	Stephen Hunter	£1.50p
☐ **Smiley's People**	John le Carré	£1.95p
☐ **To Kill a Mockingbird**	Harper Lee	£1.75p
☐ **The Empty Hours**	Ed McBain	£1.25p
☐ **Gone with the Wind**	Margaret Mitchell	£2.95p
☐ **The Totem**	Tony Morrell	£1.25p
☐ **Platinum Logic**	Tony Parsons	£1.75p
☐ **Wilt**	Tom Sharpe	£1.50p
☐ **Rage of Angels**	Sidney Sheldon	£1.75p
☐ **The Unborn**	David Shobin	£1.50p
☐ **A Town Like Alice**	Nevile Shute	£1.75p
☐ **A Falcon Flies**	Wilbur Smith	£1.95p
☐ **The Deep Well at Noon**	Jessica Stirling	£1.95p
☐ **The Ironmaster**	Jean Stubbs	£1.75p
☐ **The Music Makers**	E. V. Thompson	£1.50p

Non-fiction

☐ **Extraterrestrial Civilizations**	Isaac Asimov	£1.50p
☐ **Pregnancy**	Gordon Bourne	£2.95p
☐ **Out of Practice**	Rob Buckman	95p
☐ **The 35mm Photographer's Handbook**	Julian Calder and John Garrett	£5.95p
☐ **Travellers' Britain**	} Arthur Eperon	£2.95p
☐ **Travellers' Italy**		£2.50p
☐ **The Complete Calorie Counter**	Eileen Fowler	70p

☐	**The Diary of Anne Frank**	Anne Frank	£1.25p
☐	**Linda Goodman's Sun Signs**	Linda Goodman	£1.95p
☐	**Mountbatten**	Richard Hough	£2.50p
☐	**How to be a Gifted Parent**	David Lewis	£1.95p
☐	**Symptoms**	Sigmund Stephen Miller	£2.50p
☐	**Book of Worries**	Robert Morley	£1.50p
☐	**The Hangover Handbook**	David Outerbridge	£1.25p
☐	**The Alternative Holiday Catalogue**	edited by Harriet Peacock	£1.95p
☐	**The Pan Book of Card Games**	Hubert Phillips	£1.75p
☐	**Food for All the Family**	Magnus Pyke	£1.50p
☐	**Everything Your Doctor Would Tell You If He Had the Time**	Claire Rayner	£4.95p
☐	**Just Off for the Weekend**	John Slater	£2.50p
☐	**An Unfinished History of the World**	Hugh Thomas	£3.95p
☐	**The Third Wave**	Alvin Toffler	£1.95p
☐	**The Flier's Handbook**		£5.95p

All these books are available at your local bookshop or newsagent, or can be ordered direct from the publisher. Indicate the number of copies required and fill in the form below 6

....

Name_____
(Block letters please)

Address_____

_____

Send to Pan Books (CS Department), Cavaye Place, London SW10 9PG
Please enclose remittance to the value of the cover price plus:
35p for the first book plus 15p per copy for each additional book ordered
to a maximum charge of £1.25 to cover postage and packing
Applicable only in the UK

While every effort is made to keep prices low, it is sometimes
necessary to increase prices at short notice. Pan Books reserve
the right to show on covers and charge new retail prices which
may differ from those advertised in the text or elsewhere